Privatization in
Developing Countries

Privatization in Developing Countries

Its Impact on Economic Development and Democracy

JACQUES V. DINAVO

PRAEGER

Westport, Connecticut
London

Library of Congress Cataloging-in-Publication Data

Dinavo, Jacques Vangu.
    Privatization in developing countries : its impact on economic
development and democracy / Jacques V. Dinavo.
        p. cm.
    Includes bibliographical references and index.
    ISBN 0–275–95007–7 (alk. paper)
    1. Privatization—Developing countries.   2. Developing countries—
Economic conditions.   3. Democracy—Developing countries.
    4. Privatization—Africa, Sub-Saharan—Case studies.   I. Title.
HD4420.8.D56   1995
338.9'009172'4—dc20   94–32925

British Library Cataloguing in Publication Data is available.

Library of Congress Catalog Card Number: 94–32925
ISBN: 0–275–95007–7

First published in 1995

Praeger Publishers, 88 Post Road West, Westport, CT 06881
An imprint of Greenwood Publishing Group, Inc.

Printed in the United States of America

The paper used in this book complies with the
Permanent Paper Standard issued by the National
Information Standards Organization (Z39.48–1984).

10 9 8 7 6 5 4 3 2 1

Contents

Illustrations

FIGURE

TABLES

Foreword

This book is a tribute to an exceptionally able professor and scholar, George W. Shepherd, who has taught, guided and inspired hundreds of students at the Graduate School of International Studies (G.S.I.S.), University of Denver, and influenced thousands more through his many books and articles.

Scattered over the globe are scholars, professors, government officials, opposition leaders, workers, officers in nongovernmental organizations (NGOs) and advocates of creative change whose influence, impact and service can be traced to seeds planted by Dr. Shepherd.

I am grateful, appreciative and deeply indebted to Professor George Shepherd for his generosity, unselfishness, insights and time. He has been, and will remain, a mentor to all of us.

Preface

While I was finishing the doctorate program at the Graduate School of International Studies (G.S.I.S.), University of Denver in Colorado, my Ph.D. dissertation committee members exhorted me to keep up with current literature and to continue to conduct empirical research. This challenge initiated the work which led to the writing of this book.

My interest in privatization arises from my training in the field of international economics as well as my professional experience.

The decision to undertake this study grew out of conversations with scholars, professors, graduate students, international organization officials, corporate executives and government authorities. My wife, Dr. Trina R. Dinavo, also provided inspiration while teaching at the George Washington University's Elliott School of International Affairs.

Several studies have been done in the field of economic theories, economic development theories, development theories, socioeconomic development theory, political economy, political science, and public policy, but no studies have been done recently to assess how privatization affects economic development and democracy in the developing countries.

The central argument of *Privatization in Developing Countries: Its Impact On Economic Development and Democracy* is that privatization will bring about economic development and democracy.

The economic, social and political goals set by governments in running state-owned enterprises in the developing countries have not been realized. The public sector's economic objective of contributing to the process of development and economic growth did not materialize. In trying to meet its social goals of providing employment for its people, the public sector has become the largest employer in most developing countries, but it has been plagued with problems of mismanagement, padded payrolls, inefficiency, incompetence and noncompetitiveness. The political goal of the public sector, which consists of securing power and pride for the political elites, has been overexploited to a point where a handful of individuals, belonging to the same class and ethnic group, hold the majority of wealth in their countries and control the resources generated from state-owned enterprises.

Many policymakers recognize that most state-owned enterprises are losing money. The public sector is just not working, especially in the developing countries, particularly in Sub-Saharan Africa. Substantial sums of money are needed to subsidize these failed enterprises. Inefficiencies, poor performance, low quality of goods and services, misallocation of resources and lack of managerial skills, have caused the financing of state-owned enterprises to become a burden on government budgets.

Based on the poor record and outcome of the state-owned enterprises for the last few decades, also based on foreign aid and foreign borrowing for the last thirty-four years, the developing countries should think of how to privatize and not whether or not to privatize. The aim of privatization is to reduce the role that governments play in national economies and to encourage the private sector to take over this role.

This book seeks to demonstrate that privatization, if well implemented, will have a positive impact on economic development and democracy. Privatization is presented as a process of transfer of assets from the public sector to the private sector. The state may opt to keep all its equity and delegate the management of the enterprise to the private sector or it may choose to sell a portion of its assets and retain majority or minority ownership, establishing a joint public-private venture. Under this arrangement, the government is expected to liberalize protected markets and encourage competition. Privatization should thus increase efficiency and improve the quality of goods and services produced.

We define economic development as a process in which there is growth in the nation's economy; where there is a sustained improvement in the well-being of the people, where there is a rise in the gross national product (GNP); where the decision-making process involves a greater participation of diversified groups in a society; where the entrepreneurs play a key role in the economic growth of a nation; where the private sector, as opposed to the public sector, dominates the economy of the country, which has not been the case in many developing countries; and finally, as a process where government and private enterprises work hand in hand to improve the welfare of the people. Economic development has become a major political issue in the developing countries. Government officials are being asked by their people to alleviate poverty, to improve the system of education, and to put in place an industrial infrastructure that could bring about sustained economic growth and to raise the standard of living of the population.

One of the key ingredients to success of privatization is a democratic political system. As citizens participate freely in the privatization process, democratic institutions will be strengthened and people will have a say in the way the country's business affairs are conducted.

Chapter 1 discusses the theoretical framework of privatization. Chapter 2 discusses the theoretical framework of economic development and democracy. Chapter 3 discusses the role of the World Bank, the International Monetary Fund and the United States in privatization in developing countries. Chapter 4 deals with privatization in developing countries: theory and practice. Chapter 5 deals with the role of multinational corporations and foreign direct investment in the privatization process in developing countries. Chapter 6 discusses the case of Zaire and how state-owned enterprises have failed. Chapter 7 discusses the case of Cameroon and prospects for the success of privatization.

The last chapter discusses the question of who is to gain from privatization in developing countries: the Western world, that is, foreign investors and multinational corporations, or developing countries, that is, special interest groups, the ruling elites, ethnic groups or the population as a whole.

This book should be of interest to a wide spectrum of professionals in the following spheres: academia, private sector firms, international organizations, and government, especially middle- and high-level government personnel in the United States and abroad who play an instrumental role in shaping domestic and/or foreign policy as it relates to developing countries.

Acknowledgments

Several people and institutions deserve my appreciation and gratitude, but I could not name them all here.

Certainly, my largest debt and gratitude is to my wife, Dr. Trina R. Dinavo, a colleague and fellow student at the University of Denver, Graduate School of International Studies (G.S.I.S.), who was personally involved in editing and commenting on the manuscript from 1991 to 1993. At that time she was teaching at both the Elliott School of International Affairs and the Department of Political Science, The George Washington University. I am deeply grateful for her constructive criticism and countless hours spent reading and editing.

I would also like to express my deep gratitude to Edward A. Hawley, former executive editor of *Africa Today*, who contributed to the editing of the manuscript.

In addition, I have been coached, tutored and assisted by several reviewers, experts and scholars, to whom I am also grateful. I am also grateful for their intelligent reviews, innumerable and invaluable suggestions, additions, deletions and modifications.

I am indebted to a large number of individuals, professors, scholars, graduate students, government officials, directors of international organizations and corporate executives who have assisted me in dealing with various topics treated in this book.

My gratefulness extends also to my parents, Simon Mpaka and Engelique Twizamo Ditonua, and also to some special people, among them: George W. Shepherd, Kit Sober, Allen G. Martin, Tina Warkentin Bohn, Charles M. Ross, Henry Phillips, Jean Snyder, Jack Hall, Betty LeMaster McKean, Edward Hawley, E. Thomas Rowe, Maurice East, James Mittelman, Ved P. Nanda, David H. Bayley, Joseph Szyliowicz, Trevor Bell, Michael Fry, Henry Phillips, Robert Rycroft, Vincent Khapoya, Peter and Sheila Boulay, Gene Ellis, Elmer Newfeld, and Don Beeman.

Finally, special acknowledgment must be made to Ron and Glynnis Mileikowsky, Missy Wohlford and the staff at Greenwood Publishing Group, Inc., who rendered competent and tireless service to prepare the manuscript for publication.

A Theoretical Framework of Privatization

INTRODUCTION

In theory or in practice, very little was heard about privatization prior to the 1980s. Since then, governments of both developed and developing nations of the world have actively embraced this concept. Governments have made decisions to dispose of state-owned enterprises by either selling them to the public sector, liquidating them or going into joint venture with the private sector. Economists, political economists and political scientists have written extensively about the subject. However, most of these writers have failed to show the impact of privatization on economic development and democracy in the developing countries. This aspect of the problem has been unsatisfactorily treated by the existing literature, and we intend to shed light on this issue throughout this study.

The only known cases of privatization before the 1980s were the liquidations of the U.S. federal government's enterprises created during the Second World War. But this is not true privatization as we know it today.

Privatization in practice has, indeed, attracted much attention in Western industrialized economies as well as in the developing economies. Its aim is to reduce the role that governments play in their national economies and to encourage the private sector to take over this role for many reasons that are discussed later in this chapter.

The concept of privatization is a very sensitive one due to its economic, financial, technical, social and especially its political ramifications. Politics plays the most important role in deciding whether or not to privatize. Not only does the government have to find potential buyers but it also has to convince its people that privatization of such state-owned enterprises is in the best interest of the nation as a whole. In some cases governments are being asked to get rid of enterprises that are a burden to the taxpayers. As John Heath states: "If you can't control public enterprises to achieve efficiency, if they drain the financial resources of the state, if they absorb too much time and energy of senior politicians and civil servants, if reform is too difficult—take them out of the government."[1] Thus, many economists agree that privatization is the best means to enhance efficiency by stimulating competition.

Several governments have opted for privatization in order to maximize consumer choice, promote competition and improve quality and efficiency of the goods and services provided by the state-owned enterprises. Among the world's industrialized economies, the concept of privatization has been emphasized and applied in Great Britain where Margaret Thatcher's government made it the cornerstone of her economic policy, in the United States during the Reagan administration, and in France under François Mitterand. But in the United States, the emphasis has been more on the state and local government levels than on the federal government level.

Many governments of developing nations have also embarked on privatization programs as a means to enhance their economies. Many of these governments in Asia, Africa and Latin America are slowly but cautiously turning state-owned enterprises over to the private sector. This is because of the benefits that come with a free market economy and free enterprise spirit. Developing nations have come to realize that economic growth has been hindered by government bureaucracy and inefficiency. In many cases, state-owned enterprises have failed to improve the quality of life in the developing nations as more and more funds have been diverted to stabilize these enterprises at the expense of the people.

However, privatization has not always succeeded, and we consider some empirical examples of the failure of privatization, resulting in the flight of foreign investment and the creation of huge deficits in government budgets. We also discuss an empirical case of the success of privatization in a developing country. There are also some legal implications of privatization that make the practicality of privatization very difficult, especially in some of the developing countries where the judicial systems are not well implemented or respected by the ruling elites.

Privatization is, in fact, a complex subject and we intend to bring to this discussion the different meanings of privatization as well as shed new light on the subject.

The central argument of this book is simply stated as follows: privatization will bring economic development and democracy in the developing countries. This argument is supported throughout this book.

Economic development is also defined as a process where the gap between the rich and the poor decreases over time, a process where the entrepreneurs play a key role in the economic growth of a nation and the like. One of the measures of economic development is the gross national product (GNP). GNP is the total annual value of goods and services produced by a country. When there is an increase in GNP per capita over time, development has taken place. In addition, privatization will have a positive impact on democracy because in a democratic society, no individual is excluded from the decision-making process. Democracy is the government of the people, by the people, for the people. There is a positive relationship between capitalism and democracy. All the industrialized nations that hold economic powers, have the most committed democratic systems. When the state-owned enterprises are privatized, no one individual or one class or one ethnic group will hold all the wealth and the revenues generated from those enterprises. In the developing countries there is a need for public-private partnership. Clyde Mitchell-Weaver and Brenda Manning state that "the contemporary idea of public-private partnership as an approach to economic development has its origin in American and British public policy during the late 1970s."[2]

Theories of economics, political economy, political science, public policy and sociology have dealt with the concept of privatization and its uses. For the purpose of this discussion the terms state-owned enterprises and public enterprises are used interchangeably. Public enterprise means "public production for private consumption."[3] In order for privatization to take place there must be, among other variables, a market for it. Harvey Averch defines market as "a social arrangement that permits voluntary exchange of privately provided goods and services with known or discoverable attributes."[4] We now proceed to the different definitions of the concept of privatization.

WHAT DOES PRIVATIZATION MEAN?

Several governments throughout the world have embraced privatization in order to relieve burden on the national budget, maximize consumer choice and improve the quality of goods and services.[5] Raymond Vernon argues that a number of observers view privatization as a relaxation of government restrictions, which includes permission of minority private ownership in state-owned enterprises, the appointment of private managers to positions of managerial responsibility in state-owned enterprises and the participation of private concerns in enterprises previously considered state monopoly.[6]

And, in more general terms but quite similarly stated, Thomas Callaghy and Ernest Wilson define privatization as any action that serves to "dilute or eliminate government equity ownership or managerial control of an enterprise."[7] Callaghy and Wilson argue that this type of privatization involves the transfer of company assets from the government as owner to a private sector receiver. In order for this to be termed privatization, the government does not have to sell all its equity, it may choose to sell a portion of it to either one or several buyers as it desires. In some instances, as we see later, governments have chosen to retain ownership but opted to transfer managerial know-how to the private sector. Ravi Ramamurti argues that privatization "refers to the sale of all or part of a government's equity in state-owned enterprises (SOEs) to the private sector."[8]

Privatization as defined by Steve Hanke is a transfer of assets and service functions from public to private hands. Hanke emphasizes activities ranging from selling state-owned enterprises to contracting out public services with private contractors.[9] The concept of contracting out is highlighted when we discuss the different forms of privatization.

From an economic point of view, Calvin Kent defines privatization as the transfer of functions for which the government previously held a monopoly into the hands of the private sector. These functions are performed by the private sector at prices that clear the market and reflect the full costs of production, whereas they were performed at zero or below full-cost prices by the government.[10] Paul Starr, on the other hand, sees privatization as a policy movement and as a process that shows every sign of reconstituting major institutional domains of contemporary society. He defines privatization as a "shift of individual involvements from the whole to the part—that is, from public action to private concerns."[11] Starr goes further by defining privatization as another kind of withdrawal from the whole to the part: a transfer of ownership to the private sector of a good formerly accessible to the public sector at large.[12]

Quite similarly, Marc Bendick, Jr., defines privatization as "shifting into nongovernmental hands some or all roles in producing a good or service that was once publicly produced or might be publicly produced."[13] In discussing privatization, T. Kolderie argues that governments perform two separate functions, either of which—or both—could be privatized.[14] The first function he identifies is provision and the second one is production. Production is the administrative action to produce that good and service, whereas provision is the policy decision to provide a good or service.

David Donnison takes a different angle in defining privatization stating that privatization is a word that has been coined by politicians and disseminated by political journalists. The proponents and opponents of privatization have used this concept to mobilize support from their own side and dramatize a conflict. Dennison argues that the meaning of privatization is at best uncertain and biased.[15]

However, in keeping with the general consensus, Michael O'Higgins defines privatization as a term that describes the reduction of the role that the state plays in supplying goods and services to the population.[16] A. Walker sees privatization not only as an attempt to differentiate between public and private sources but also as a means of striking a new balance between them, particularly in the wake of changes in public-sector services.[17] V. V. Ramanadham argues that in the United Kingdom the idea that privatization most prominently suggests is "denationalization (in the sense of transferring the ownership of a public enterprise to private hands). Another idea in vogue is liberalization and deregulation, which unleash forces of competition."[18] Paul Cook and Colin

Kirkpatrick see privatization as a range of different policy initiatives intended to change the balance between the public and private sector and the services they provide.[19] They distinguish three main approaches to privatization: a change in the ownership of the enterprise, liberalization or deregulation and a transfer of good or service from the public to private sector while the government retains ultimate responsibility for supplying the service.

We commonly view privatization as a process of transfer of assets from the public sector to the private sector. The state may opt to keep all its equity and delegate the management of the enterprise to the private sector or it may chose to sell a portion of its assets and retain majority or minority ownership, in other words, establishing a joint venture between the public and the private sectors. Under this privatization arrangement, the government is expected to liberalize protected markets and encourage competition. Privatization is thus assumed to increase efficiency and improve the quality of goods and services produced.

There are different forms of privatization and there are several reasons why governments chose to privatize state-owned enterprises. There are some advantages and disadvantages to privatization as we see later on. The pros and cons of privatization are discussed later in this chapter. Privatization is not only an economic, financial and social issue, but it is also a very sensitive domestic and political issue, especially in the developing countries where potential buyers within a particular country are limited because they do not have buying power.

We are most interested in exploring the impact of privatization on economic development and democracy in the developing countries. Does privatization promote economic development and democracy? What are the advantages of privatization? Can privatization cause political conflict and ethnic division in a nation? Who is to gain from privatization? In this book, we look at some empirical case studies dealing with issues. But at this point we want to identify the different forms of privatization.

There are, indeed, many issues involved in privatization. How does a newly privatized enterprise proceed to achieve the national, social, economic and political objectives set up by the government? Is privatization a panacea for developing countries?[20] How does the government ensure that new private investors will be able to sustain these private enterprises? And how does the government ensure that there will be distribution of wealth among the nationals? And who will be the new buyers or investors? If the majority ownership of the newly privatized enterprise is held by foreign investors, how can they be ensured that these enterprises will not be subject to nationalization by the governments? How would the population treat these foreign investors? Will their involvement be considered a form of neo-colonialism? If the buyers of the newly privatized enterprises consist of a handful of ruling elites belonging to a small class within the society, would this create ethnic conflict, especially in developing countries?

PRIVATIZATION: ITS VARIOUS FORMS

Some material that lists forms of privatization has been produced by the World Bank in the form of working papers. In this book, we look into the pros and cons of each form. Under what conditions is one form feasible or desirable, vis-à-vis another form? Under what conditions might privatization have negative political or economic consequences? These are questions that we intend to treat in this study. Privatization is a measure that has been implemented by several governments worldwide in both developed and developing countries. There are different forms of privatization in different countries. Whatever form of privatization is chosen, no government should continue to allow itself to produce goods and services for its population. This did not work in the former Soviet Union. It also has proven to be a failure in the former Eastern European bloc and is proving fatal to the Cuban economy and in other countries where the government still holds monopoly ownership of the economy. R. and P. Musgrave argues that the provision of goods and services by the state should be limited to those instances in which goods and services are clearly of a public or collective nature.[21]

There are many different forms of privatization. Harry Hatry conducted a survey that lists different forms of privatization such as subsidies, grants, franchises, contracting out, self-help, volunteers, use of regulatory and taxing authority, reducing the demand for service, obtaining temporary help from the private sector, forming ventures between the public and private sectors.[22]

There are eight commonly used forms of privatization in the industrialized developed and developing nations:

1. contracting out;
2. voucher;
3. sales of assets by the government to private sector: joint venture;
4. subsidies;
5. load-shedding;
6. private payment;
7. management privatization; and
8. liberalization or deregulation.

Contracting Out

The first and simplest form of privatization[23] is contracting out. This type of privatization is widely used.[24] This is the principal form of privatization in the United States. William Gormley, Jr., points out that "99 percent of all local governments have contracted out services over the past five years; 96 percent expect to contract out services in the next two years."[25]

Contracting out is also commonly used in the developing countries where the private sector is involved in the provision of certain goods and services but the government remains in charge of all major activities. Calvin Kent cautions that promoters of contracting with the private sector often tend to charge excessive fees for their services. He argues that very little has been achieved if "contracting involves nothing more than the exchange of a private monopoly for a governmental one."[26] He also adds that exclusive contracts should be avoided when possible, since one of the virtues of privatization is to allow competition to take place, and, this is accomplished by an open door policy to all entrepreneurs in the private sector.

The pros of this form of privatization are that it allows the entrepreneurs to compete in the marketplace. Contracting out creates jobs in the private sector. The con of contracting out is that in the developing countries, government officials and ruling elites tend to give the contracts to their business associates, friends and family members. During our research, we found this to be the case in Malaysia, Indonesia, Kenya, Zaire, Côte d'Ivoire, Peru and Chile. Thus this form of privatization might have negative political and economic consequences, if the contractors are unable to deliver the desired goods and services to the consumers.

Voucher

As far as public programs are concerned, a voucher is nothing more than a transfer of income to a citizen in order to increase that individual's ability to purchase a good or service.[27] In using the voucher the consumer has a choice among the goods and services produced at a lower cost. In other words, the consumer is authorized to purchase earmarked goods or services from the private market. In the United States, the leading example of this voucher privatization is the food stamp program. The government determines the providers of the services and the users of the services.[28]

This form of privatization is not commonly used in the developing countries. It has been tried in Russia, but there were several abuses where some wealthy individuals were purchasing these vouchers from the people for their own benefit. Since with this form of privatization the government specifies who is eligible to purchase the services and who is eligible to provide them, the chances for government officials to choose their friends and relatives are enormous.

Sales of Assets or Equity: Joint Venture

Divestiture is a total sale of all or part of the company to private investors.[29] There is an actual change of ownership of an enterprise from the public to private sector.

This raises an interesting issue because there does not seem to be too much of a problem in the developed industrialized countries where capital markets are well organized and developed. Equity could be easily sold to the public because of the buying power of the people. Margaret Thatcher's administration in Great Britain carried out this form of privatization successfully in the cases of British Aerospace, British National Oil, Jaguar, Amersham and National Freight Consortium.[30]   In the United States is concerned, only "24 percent of local governments have sold some assets to private buyers over the past five years, and only 21 percent expect to do so in the next two years. At the federal level, Conrail and some government loan portfolios have been sold but proposals to sell Amtrak, the Naval Petroleum Reserves and other assets have not gone far."[31]

However, the sale of equity, in whole or in part, is a very tedious task and a very sensitive issue in the developing countries where capital markets either are nonexistent or undeveloped. In certain instances where this form of privatization has been adopted there were some severe economic, social and political problems, as we discover later.

The sale of equity could also take place in the form of a joint venture between the government and the private sector where the government could hold majority or minority ownership. Cook and Kirkpatrick discuss this aspect of privatization as denationalization and divestiture. Denationalization could involve the sale of the enterprise as a complete entity or as a joint venture between the public and private sectors. In extreme cases, they argue, "divestiture may involve the abandonment or formal liquidation of the state-owned enterprise."[32]   Kent points out that taxpayer revolts during the late 1960s and the early 1970s resulted in the acceleration of privatization in the United States at the state and local levels.[33]   C. F. Valente and L. D. Manchester authored a report that shows the privatization in whole or in part of over sixty local government functions.[34]   We would also argue that privatization serves the public interest.[35]

The pros of this form of privatization in the developing countries are the lack of developed capital markets in most of the developing countries. This form of privatization brings about some severe economic, social and political problems in some developing countries. In the case of privatizing strategic industries such as oil, mining and transportation, government officials may be accused of selling the national interest to foreign investors and this can result in political demonstrations, sabotage, destruction of economic and transportation infrastructures. This has been recently the case with Gecamines in Zaire, as it was the case with the copper mines in Chile and the oil industry in Algeria.

Subsidies

Subsidies are designed to provide profit opportunities to private firms by "subsidizing some of their production inputs—those the governmental sector would like to see employed."[36] This is a very common form of privatization in the developing countries. The con of this form of privatization is that it drains scarce government funds, causing major budget deficits. This form of privatization should be avoided in the developing countries. It has negative political and economic consequences. Under these conditions, the sales of assets or equity might be more feasible vis-à-vis subsidies.

Load-Shedding

Load-shedding deals with involves the government abandoning some activity, which may or may not be picked up by the private sector, depending on the nature of the activity and the need in the community.[37]

With this form of privatization the private sector decides whether to get involved when the government, for instance in the United States, cuts back some welfare programs, or any other programs that are cut by the administration. This type of privatization is very rare in the developing countries.

Several scholars have argued that load-shedding makes the distribution of income more unequal. Evelyn Brodkin and Dennis Young argue that the inequality of income and wealth between the haves and the have-nots increases when government's role as a provider of services that benefit mainly the have-nots is minimized.[38]

The con with this form of privatization is that it increases the inequalities in income and wealth in a society. It widens the gap between the haves and the have-nots.

Private Payment

Private payment for public service is another form of privatization. With this option, the government still provides the service. User fees are the means by which the full cost of the service is paid by the public.[39] This form of privatization should not be recommended in the developing countries. The con with private payment is that the public may wind up paying more for the services.

Liberalization or Deregulation

The liberalization or deregulation of entry into activities previously restricted to public sector enterprises is another form of privatization.[40]   This form removes all or some restrictions in entering a particular market in order to increase competition, hence giving more choices to the consumer. The advantages of this form of privatization are that it increases competition in the marketplace and increases choices to the consumer.

Government officials in many Sub-Saharan African countries still refuse to liberalize the import/export business.   This helps these officials, their friends, relatives and business associates to keep the monopoly on these businesses. During our research, we found this to be the case in Zaire, Mozambique, Tanzania, Benin, Gabon, Kenya, Zambia, Angola, Mali, Peru and Indonesia. Liberalization of import/export industry, for instance, could help promote competition and thus stabilize the prices of imported goods in the marketplace and thus diffuse political tensions between privileged groups and the majority of the people.

Management Privatization

In the case of management privatization, the private sector, with its expertise and know-how, is invited by the government to take over the management of a particular state-owned enterprise.   However, under the agreement, the government still retains complete ownership of the state-owned enterprise. Under this management privatization, it is questionable whether the state maintains control of the enterprise. This form of privatization has been adopted in Malaysia and elsewhere.

This form of privatization should be used often in the developing countries. The pro is that the private sector, in most instances, has more expertise and know-how in a particular industry than the public sector. The con is that the government is always looking over the private sector's shoulder since complete ownership remains with the government. Conflicts between the government and the private sector in charge may produce negative consequences. The private sector may be forced to produce goods and services whose quality may not be desirable to the customers, and it may be forced to terminate the contract at an early date.

This leads us to the next important and relevant question: Why privatization?

WHY PRIVATIZATION? THEORY AND PRACTICE

Many policymakers throughout the world have realized that most state-owned enterprises are losing money. The public sector is just not working, especially in the developing countries. States have been spending substantial sums of money to subsidize these enterprises. Gray Cowan argues that industries can be managed more effectively and goods and services rendered more efficiently by private than by the government, and at lower cost to the public.[41] Many international institutions and organizations such as the International Bank for Reconstruction and Development (The World Bank), the International Monetary Fund (IMF) as well as the most industrialized nations such as the United States, have opted for privatization as a urgent policy, in particular for the developing countries. Ramanadham argues that the inefficiency of enterprise managers, causes losses, which for some reason, cannot be remedied. The cause of losses could be eliminated through privatization since, by hypothesis, "a private enterprise works for profit and closes if losses persist."[42] He argues that whenever a public enterprise no longer holds its comparative advantage it is preferable to privatize it. Ramanadham goes on by arguing that a state-owned enterprise should be reorganized into a private enterprise when it has a comparative disadvantage in making a contribution to the national well-being. Alternatively, public enterprise should be preferred to other forms if it proves to be a superior means of making a contribution to the national well-being.[43] He argues that commercial returns, social returns and a desired trade-off between them, ought to be the measures of this comparative advantage. In many instances, entrepreneurs are being asked to rescue the ailing state-owned enterprises.[44]

Raymond Vernon talks about cases of gross incompetence, padded payrolls, and even outright looting of state-owned enterprises. He states that "flagrant instances under each of these headings have appeared in various countries, including the Philippines, Indonesia, Nigeria, and Zaire."[45] We elaborate on this point later with an empirical case study in this research work.

In discussing state-owned enterprises in the developed countries, Vernon argues the case of the British Government, where external financial limits were placed on its various enterprises making that tool the centerpiece of its control systems.[46] Explicit contracts were drawn between the French Government and its principal state-owned enterprises, which defined the limits of external borrowing and claims on the national budget.[47] He concludes that all such measures, however, proved flawed. Once the necessary financial controls were in place, governments still could not refrain from making demands on their state-owned enterprises to hold down prices, raise wages or keep idle workers on the payroll—demands that made the financial controls inoperative or ineffective.[48]

Stuart Butler holds that public responsibilities can be discharged more efficiently and more effectively by the private sector than the public sector. These public responsibilities include education, transportation, the protection of environment and other sectors. However, Butler is concerned about the contracting out form of privatization. He cautions that this may result in the creation of new constituencies that favor increased levels of government expenditures. He expresses the same concern with the voucher form, arguing that those private enterprises who have benefited from vouchers are likely to develop a powerful lobby that favors increased government spending. He concludes by warning that the "size and cost of government are not automatically reduced by privatization."[49]

In discussing privatization as theory and rhetoric, Paul Starr talks about two normative theories that justify privatization as a direction for public policy. These theories draw their inspiration, he argues, from several different visions of a good society. He contends that "the vision grounded in laissez-faire individualism and free-market economies that promises greater efficiency, a smaller government, and more individual choice if only we expand the domain of property rights and market forces."[50] In contrast, Starr puts forth a second vision, which is steeped in conservative thinking and promulgates reliance and strength built up on families, churches and large nonprofit organizations—the backbone of powerbase of communities.[51] Concurring with Starr, Peter Berger and Richard Neuhaus[52] see privatization as community development. They propose that government give more power to community organizations, voluntary associations, churches and self-help groups. Government and state must change their role in the development process.[53]

Another theory that justifies privatization states that demands on the state will likely be reduced and deflected through privatization. Simply stated, proponents of privatization believe that employees' wage claims from the public treasury should be diverted to private employers.[54] How will this work? Ideally, as Starr suggests, the answer is "a trickle-down of entrepreneurship from the newly privatized managers to the workers; for that very reason, privatizers often are perfectly willing to sell to the workers at an advantageous price whole enterprises or at least some portion of the shares."[55] Starr sees also the privatization of public assets and enterprises as a privatization of wealth. He gives an example of the Margaret Thatcher administration's privatization policy as a policy designed to increase the proportion of the population who are shareholders of the privatized enterprises. In this case the emphasis is put on the profit generated by these enterprises. In general, however, Starr is very critical of privatization, which he characterizes as self-defeating. He argues that privatization will, indeed, undermine the compensation it claims to promote. He believes that privatization will promote a much greater public regulation of the private sector. Brodkin and Young argue that there are two other mechanisms that remain for changing the distribution of income and wealth. These are the private marketplace and charitable giving. Based on the economic theory, charitable giving mechanisms are likely to be weak substitutes for government actions while the private marketplace is likely to be regressive.[56]

Discussing privatization in Great Britain, Yair Aharoni maintains the political view of the socialists in Great Britain who believes that a just economic system and an ideal society based on cooperation, equality and mutual collaboration could be created automatically by state ownership.[57]   As was the case in the developed and developing countries, the public expected the state-owned enterprises to provide the service these enterprises were supposed to provide regardless of whether or not they made profits and the workers also believed that "regardless of whether they are earned"[58] their wages should be paid.

Raymond Vernon argues that for privately owned factories and shipyards that were not performing well, state-owned enterprises in both developed and developing countries were often expected to come to their rescue.   In brief, policies of governments, rather than their own inefficiencies, were the cause of deficits of the state-owned enterprises.[59]   These governments in the developed and developing countries failed to reach their goals of promoting growth and development through state-owned enterprises.   Resources in most cases were being diverted from accomplishing these aims of rescuing failed enterprises of the private sector.   In most cases governments wound up inheriting failed enterprises from the private sector.   This increased the burden of government budgets.   Governments opted for privatization due to the failure to achieve the goals that they had set through the operation of state-owned enterprises.[60]

Another phenomenon that has increased the interest of some governments in privatization has been the fact that many state-owned enterprises tend to fall under the dominance of one or more of the principal stockholders.[61]   In developing countries, the principal shareholders are usually the ruling ethnic groups, who get richer at the expense of the masses.   As we see in the case of privatization in the developing countries, this is a major point of concern since wealth is concentrated mainly in the hands of a few ruling elites and the majority of the population do not have the capital to acquire shares of the newly privatized enterprises.   This may have adverse economic and political implications.   One thing is clear: the principal goal of privatization in both developed and developing countries is to shrink the size of government expenditures and promote competition and efficiency in the goods and services produced.

Janet Rothenberg Pack[62] identifies three related but not identical goals of privatization that dominate the discussion: to reduce the size of the government sector (i.e., the ratio of government expenditure to GNP), to reduce the federal budget deficit (to reduce government expenditures minus government revenues in the short term) and to increase the efficiency of public service delivery (i.e., increase the real output for a given level of government expenditure.   According to the supporters of privatization, the private sector can do a much better job than the public sector.   More specifically, they argue that there is a likelihood for public bureaucracies to fail.[63]   Many opponents of privatization concede the failures of public bureaucracies, but acknowledge that institutional redesign is a means through which public bureaucracies could be enhanced.[64]   Other scholars have raised the question whether privatization is the answer.[65]

There has been a rapid growth of government in the last twenty years and privatization is a response to stopping this growth.   Elliot Berg argues that in the early 1970s, "thirteen countries were spending close to 30 percent of their GNP in the public sector; by the end of the decade about forty countries were spending more than a third of their GNP in the public sector."[66]   In the developing countries, state-owned enterprises account for 10 to 20 percent of GNP. This is one of the reasons privatization is believed to be the remedy for the developing countries. In developing countries, state-owned enterprises are now responsible for between 20 and 60 percent of total investment spending.[67]

Peter McPherson states that by eliminating the costly subsidies that governments pay to keep inefficient parastatals running, privatization has helped reduce government deficits.[68]   Privatization is the best means to respond to consumer demands and needs. Due to the competition it creates in the free market, privatization also helps improve the quality of the goods and services produced in the market. These enterprises, which provide the best quality of goods and services, will survive in the market since the competition among the producers is keen. This is the case in the developed and developing countries. As quality of goods and services increase, which satisfy the needs and demands of the consumers, these consumers will purchase these goods and services. This increases demand to produce more goods and services and hence creates jobs. This helps the growth of the economies of both developed and developing countries. The question of privatization in the developing countries is discussed in more detail in a subsequent chapter.

Opponents and Proponents of Privatization

There have been proponents and opponents of privatization among scholars as well as the practitioners. In general, labor unions have been the strongest opponents of privatization. Steve Lord states that the labor unions "have shown the determination to resist the onslaught on their jobs and services and fight the threat of privatization."[69]   If privatization is successful, the labor unions should not worry about the loss of jobs; as a matter of fact, as we argued earlier, as the market economies are strengthened through increases in incomes and revenues due to the increase in the quality of goods and services for the consumers, demand for these goods and services will increase, which creates new jobs. This is not to say that we cannot find failed attempts at privatization in the developing world. However, we fully understand the concern of labor unions regarding the loss of jobs since state-owned enterprises are often the largest employers. This is especially true in the developing countries. Therefore, it is unlikely that a newly privatized firm will keep all the employees that were on the payroll when the firm operated as a public enterprise.

There are several arguments against privatization. One such argument is that social and regional obligations of the citizens may no longer be achieved by privatized companies taken over by foreign investors.[70]   This argument is hard to prove since in many countries where privatization has taken place the governments exercise the same influence and power over these privatized enterprises as over those that are state owned. There may be some instances where foreign investors of newly privatized firms dictate the policy of their new firms, especially in the developing countries. Still, the governments of these countries have more influence over these industries through laws, duties, royalties, and profits transferred abroad.

On the other hand, proponents of privatization argue that privatization helps increase the number of shareholders. For instance in the case of Great Britain, from 1979 to 1988 the number of shareholders tripled. In practically all cases, argues Aharoni, since privatization investments, sales and profits have skyrocketed. These results proven the "inherent inferiority of state-owned firms."[71] Equalizing the number of stockholders of the United States, the number of shareholders among the adults in Great Britain grew from "9 percent in 1983 to 21 percent in 1987."[72] Of course one has to remember that these two countries, Great Britain and the United States, are developed industrialized countries where the population has the buying power to purchase shares. In contrast, in the developing countries, as we will discuss, the sale of stocks causes major political and ethnic problems since only a handful of government officials, often belonging to the same party or ethnic group, have the ability to buy shares in the newly privatized firms. Hence, there is no appreciable distribution of wealth, which proponents of privatization argue is supposed to occur.

As one can see, the concept of privatization is not all one-sided. Privatization is linked with political and economic problems.[73] Some opponents of privatization have also expressed that privatization creates loss of jobs and price increases, especially if the governmental function has been provided at zero or low cost. Therefore, privatization may be viewed as unfair unless it is accompanied by some form of voucher system.[74]

We talked about the different forms of privatization earlier in this chapter. One of the most commonly used forms of privatization beside sales of assets, is contracting out. However, the contracting out form of privatization does not necessarily lower the costs of goods and services.[75] The proponents of privatization argue that the prices would be lower in newly privatized companies because of the competition from many of these newly privatized firms, which may lower the prices of goods and services produced.

In addition, many proponents of privatization emphasize efficiency. They see privatization as a means to improve the quality of goods and services, decrease unit costs and increase efficiency. Others hope privatization will cut government expenditures and raise cash by selling stocks in order to reduce national and international debt.[76] Still others see it as the most important ingredient of human development and economic growth. A large group sees in privatization a way to broaden the base of ownership and participation in a society—"encouraging larger numbers to feel they have a stake in the system."[77] This was the case in Great Britain for instance when the Thatcher administration privatized a few state-owned firms.

In the debate on privatization, neoclassical analysis translates into policy prescriptions directed toward reducing the size of state-owned enterprises, removing government controls and regulations, encouraging competition and relying on the market and price mechanism to allocate resources.[78] This is especially true in the case of many developing countries where the public sector is too large and is the largest employer. All this drains the government's financial resources.

Privatization of firms can raise very sensitive questions of sovereignty and security when the enterprises to be privatized are of economic significance and strategic and military importance. For instance, in 1992 Boris Yeltsin was willing to privatize half of the state-owned enterprises involved in light industry, food processing, construction and retail services. However, Yeltsin argues that Russia will never relinquish "control of forestry and water resources, cultural treasures, gold reserves, military property and all basic infrastructure for transportation, energy production and communication."[79] The same logic applies to the oil producing countries such as Saudi Arabia. Despite the emphasis on privatization in Saudi Arabia, for instance, "there was considerable doubt that any of the profitable enterprises would be privatized."[80] Any sale of the strategic state-owned enterprises in developed or developing countries will cause a political stir.

In discussing the pros and cons of privatization Gormley states the point of view of supporters of privatization and that of its critics. He argues that to supporters, privatization scales back the public sector by increasing its reliance on the private marketplace for the delivery of goods and services to the public.[81]
In the case of the critics, "privatization conjures up visions of a beleaguered government bureaucracy ceding responsibility for vital public services to unreliable private entrepreneurs."[82] However, in defense of privatization, Gormley concludes that if well implemented, privatization can reduce government expenditures and improve the quality of goods and services.[83]

As we have seen so far, privatization is indeed a very complex issue. In this section we discussed the arguments for and against privatization. One of the main objectives of privatization is to promote competition and efficiency and we are about to discuss these concepts.

Competition and Efficiency

Most professional economists have agreed that privatization, if well carried out, leads to competition and achieves much greater efficiency and produces a much better quality of goods and services than the state-owned enterprises. Most scholars of privatization have emphasized cutting the size of government budgets by privatizing the state-owned enterprises. Competition is crucially important to stimulate efficiency. Vernon argues that the "threat of entry is sufficient to inhibit firms from earning monopoly rents."[84]

In evaluating privatization there are some important criteria that need to be looked at, including competition, efficiency, quality, reliability, accountability and legitimacy. Privatization does create competition in the markets in which the newly privatized enterprises operate. As competition increases, it enhances quality and improves performance. Competition ensures the highest quality at the lowest prices. According to Smith, competition is "an invisible hand that caused producers, while they pursued their own self-interests, to maximize the well-being of all."[85] Entrepreneurs are driven by desire to generate profits and produce better quality of goods and services to satisfy consumer demands. They have a competitive advantage over viers on the marketplace by finding a cheaper way to produce the goods and services.[86]

In contrast, the state-owned enterprises are not usually driven by the desire to make profit and do not face any competition with other firms. This is the case especially in the developing countries. Instead, managers of these state-owned enterprises are more interested in the size of their budgets and the number of employees and not necessarily with the efficiency and the quality of goods and services they provide to the consumers. In the marketplace where competition exists among firms, the consumers can choose the quality and price of the product they intend to purchase to their satisfaction. In certain countries, competition is either among newly privatized firms or between the private sector and the public sector. In any case, consumers still choose the product or services that they are satisfied with.

We must emphasize that any privatization without a policy is doomed to failure. There must be well-qualified staff to take over the management of the newly privatized firms and a well-trained labor force that will produce products with the highest quality at lower costs in the competitive marketplace. Charles Wolf[87] identifies some factors that lead to shortcomings and inefficiency: inadequacy of governmental provision, internalities and redundant and rising costs.

Our main aim in this section is to support the fact that privatization promotes competition in the marketplace and improves efficiency and quality at lower costs to the maximization of consumer satisfaction. This is the economic approach to privatization in regard to competition, efficiency and quality.

Does privatization in the developing countries have an impact on economic development and democracy? Our thesis for this book is that privatization does have an impact on economic development and democracy. This question is answered as we go along. But, in order to see whether or not there is an impact, we need to understand fully what economic development and democracy mean and what they are. And so, Chapter 2 discusses the theoretical framework of economic development and democracy.

NOTES

1. John Heath, ed., *Public Enterprises at the Crossroads: Essays in Honour of V.V. Ramanadham* (New York: Routledge, 1990), 13.

2. Clyde Mitchell-Weaver and Brenda Manning, "Public-Private Partnerships in Third World Development: A Conceptual Overview," *Studies in Comparative International Development* 26 (Winter 1991–1992): 45.

3. Leroy P. Jones, Pankaj Tandon, Ingo Vogelsang, *Selling Public Enterprises: A Cost-Benefit Methodology* (Cambridge, Mass.: The MIT Press, 1990), 1.

4. Harvey Averch, *Private Markets and Public Intervention: A Primer for Policy Designers* (Pittsburgh, Pa.: University of Pittsburgh Press, 1990), 26.

5. William T. Gormley, Jr., ed., *Privatization and Its Alternatives* (Madison: University of Wisconsin Press, 1991), 3.

6. Raymond Vernon, ed., *The Promise of Privatization: A Challenge For U.S. Policy* (New York: Council on Foreign Relations Books, 1988), 2.

7. Thomas M. Callaghy and Ernest J. Wilson III, "Africa: Policy, Reality or Ritual?" in *The Promise of Privatization: A Challenge to U.S. Policy*, ed., Raymond Vernon (New York: Council on Foreign Relations Books, 1988), 180.

8. Ravi Ramamurti, "Why Are Developing Countries Privatizing?" *Journal of International Studies* 23 (1992): 225.

9. Steve H. Hanke, ed., *Privatization and Development* (San Francisco:International Center For Economic Growth Press, 1987), 4.

10. Calvin A. Kent, "Privatization of Public Functions: Promises and Problems," in *Entrepreneurship and the Privatizing of Government*, ed. Calvin A. Kent (New York: Quorum Books, 1987), 4.

11. Paul Starr, "The Meaning of Privatization," in *Privatization and the Welfare State*, eds. Sheila B. Kamerman and Alfred J. Kahn (Princeton, N.J.: Princeton University Press, 1989), 15.

12. Ibid., 18.

13. Marc Bendick, Jr., "Privatizing the Delivery of Social Welfare Services: An Idea to be Taken Seriously," in *Privatization and the Welfare State*, eds. Sheila B. Kamerman and Alfred J. Kahn (Princeton, N.J.: Princeton University Press, 1989), 98.

14. T. Kolderie, "The Two Different Concepts of Privatization," *Public Administrative Review* (July/August 1986): 285–290.

15. David Donnison, "The Progressive Potential of Privatization," cited in Michael O'Higgins, "Social Welfare and Privatization: The British Experience," in *Privatization and the Welfare State*, eds. Sheila B. Karmerman and Alfred J. Kahn (Princeton, N.J.: Princeton University Press, 1989), 157.

16. Ibid., 157.

17. A. Walker, "The Political Economy of Privatization," in *Privatization and The Welfare State*, eds. Sheila B. Karmerman and Alfred J. Kahn (Princeton, N.J.: Princeton University Press, 1989), 159.

18. V. V. Ramanadham, ed., *Privatization in Developing Countries* (London: Routledge, 1989), 4.

19. Paul Cook and Colin Kirkpatrick, *Privatization in Less Developed Countries* (New York: St. Martin's Press, 1988), 3.

20. See, Jonas Prayer, "Is Privatization a Panacea for LDCs? Market Failure versus Public Sector Failures," *Journal of Developing Areas* 26 (April 1992): 301–321.

21. R. Musgrave and P. Musgrave, *Public Finance in Theory and Practice* (New York: McGraw-Hill, 1984), 47–67. See also Calvin A. Kent, ed. *Entrepreneurship and the Privatizing of Government* (New York: Quorum Books, 1987), 13.

22. Harry Hatry, *A Review of Private Approaches for Delivery of Public Services* (Washington, D.C.: Urban Institute, 1983), 10–100.

23. Bendik, "Privatizing the Delivery of Social Welfare Services," 106.

24. John J. Kerlin, John C. Ries, and Sidney Sonenblum, "Alternatives to City Departments," in *Alternatives for Delivering Public Services*, ed. E. S. Savas (Boulder, Colo.: Westview Press, 1977), 111–145.

25. Gormley, *Privatization and Its Alternatives*, 4.

26. Kent, *Entrepreneurship and the Privatizing of Government*, 14.

27. Bendik, "Privatizing the Delivery of social Welfare Services," 109.

28. Gormley, *Privatization and its Alternatives*, 4.

29. Kent, *Entrepreneurship and the Privatizing of Government*, 13.

30. Peter Hennessy, *Whitehall* (New York: Free Press, 1989), 501.

31. Gormley, *Privatization and Its Alternatives*, 5.

32. Cook and Kirkpatrick, *Privatization in Less Developing Countries*, 3.

33. Kent, *Entrepreneurship and the Privatizing of Government*, 5.

34. C. F. Valente and L. D. Manchester, *Rethinking Local Services: Examining Alternatives Delivery Approaches* (Chicago: Management Information Service Special Report, International City Management Association, 1984), XV.

35. See, John B. Goodman and Gary W. Loveman, "Does Privatization Serve the Public Interest?" *Harvard Business Review* 69 (November-December 1991): 26–28.

36. Bendick, "Privatizing the Delivery of Social Welfare Services," 111.

37. Gormley, *Privatization and its Alternatives*, 5.

38. Evelyn Z. Brodkin and Dennis Young, "Making Sense of Privatization: What Can We Learn from Economic and Political Analysis?" in *Privatization and the Welfare State*, eds. Sheila B. Kamerman and Alfred J. Kahn (Princeton, N.J.: Princeton University Press, 1989), 122.

39. Kent, *Entrepreneurship and the Privatizing of Government*, 15.

40. Cook and Kirkpatrick, *Privatization in Less Developing Countries*, 4.

41. L. Gray Cowan, "A Global Overview of Privatization," in *Privatization and Development*, ed. Steve H. Hanke (San Francisco: International Center for Economic Growth Press, 1987), 7.

42 Ramanadham, *Privatization in Developing Countries*, 11.

43. Ibid., 14–15.

44. See, Albert G. Holzinger, "Entrepreneurs to the Rescue," *Nation's Business* 80 (August 1992), 20–28.

45. Vernon, *The Promise of Privatization: A Challenge For U.S. Policy*, 4.

46. Ibid.

47. Ibid.

48. Ibid.

49. Stuart Butler, "Privatization for Public Purposes," *in Privatization and Its Alternatives*, ed. William T. Gormley, Jr. (Madison: University of Wisconsin Press, 1991), 17–24.

50. Starr, "The Meaning of Privatization," 26.

51. Ibid.

52. Peter L. Berger, and Richard John Neuhaus, *To Empower People: The Role of Mediating Structures in Public Policy* (Washington, D.C.: American Enterprise Institute, 1977), 36–37.

53. See also, Arturo Israel, "The Changing Role of the State in Development" *Finance & Development* 28 (June 1991), 41-43

54. Starr, "The Meaning of Privatization," 36.

55. Ibid.

56. Evelyn Z. Brodkin and Dennis Young, "Making Sense of Privatization," 123.

57. Yair Aharoni, "The United Kingdom: Transforming Attitudes," in *The Promise of Privatization: A Challenge for U.S. Foreign Policy*, ed. Ramond Vernon (New York: Council on Foreign Relations Books, 1988), 27.

58. Richard Pryke, *The Nationalized Industries: Policies and Performance Since 1968* (Oxford: Robert Martin, 1981), 265.

59. Vernon, *The Promise of Privatization: A Challenge of U.S. Policy*, 4.

60. Ibid., 10.

61. Ibid., 12.

62. Janet Rothenberg Pack, "The Opportunities and Constraints of Privatization," in *Privatization and Its Alternatives*, ed. William T. Gormley (Madison: University of Wisconsin Press, 1991), 284.

63. Gormley, Jr., *Privatization and Its Alternatives*, 6.

64. Ibid.

65. Richard Hemming and Ali M. Mansoor, "Is Privatization the Answer?" *Finance & Development* 25 (September 1988): 31–33.

66. Elliot Berg, "The Role of Divestiture in Economic Growth," in *Privatization and Development*, ed. Steve Hanke (San Francisco: International Center for Economic Growth Press, 1987), 23.

67. Ibid., 24.

68. Peter M. McPherson, "The Promise of Privatization," in *Privatization And Development*, ed. Steve H. Hanke (San Francisco: International Center for Economic Growth Press, 1987), 18.

69. Steve Lord, "Gas and Electricity Shops," in *Privatization?* eds. Sue Hastings and Hugo Levie (Oxford: Spokesman Books, 1983), 107.

70. Yair Aharoni, "The United Kingdom: Transforming Attitudes," 47.

71. Ibid., 48.

72. Ibid., 49–50.

73. For discussion of these problems, see R. Poole, Jr., "Objections to Privatization," *Policy Review* (Spring 1983): 106–121.

74. Kent, "Privatization of Public Functions: Promises and Problems," 17.

75. S. M. Butler, *Privatizing Federal Spending: A Strategy to Eliminate the Deficit* (New York: Universe Books, 1985), 56.

76. Hanke, *Privatization and Development*, 3.

77. Ibid., 4.

78. Cook and Kirkpatrick, *Privatization in Less Developing Countries*, 9.

79. Michael Dobbs, "Russia Yeltsin Reviles Communist Past, Pledges Better Life for All Within a Year," *Washington Post* 30 December 1991, 10.

80. Waheb A. Soufi and Richard T. Meyer, *Saudi Arabian Industrial Investment: An Analysis of Government-Business Relationships* (New York: Quorum Books, 1991), 113.

81. Gormley, *Privatization and Its Alternatives*, 3.

82. Ibid.

83. Ibid.

84. Vernon, *The Promise of Privatization: A Challenge for U.S. Policy*, 37.

85. A. Smith, R. H. Campbell, and W. B. Todd, eds. *An Inquiry into the Causes of the Wealth of Nations* (London: Liberty Classics, 1976), 456.

86. Kent, *Entrepreneurship and the Privatizing of Government*, 11.

87. Charles Wolf, Jr., "A Theory of Nonmarket Failure: Framework for Implementation Analysis," *Journal of Law and Economics* 4 (1979): 107–139.

2

Theoretical Framework of Economic Development and Democracy

INTRODUCTION

Several studies have been done in the field of economic development theories, development theory[1] and socioeconomic development theory.[2] But no studies have been done recently to assess how privatization affects economic development and democracy in the developing countries. We intend to shed light on this issue of critical importance in today's world.

What Does Economic Development Mean?

After reading the work of several scholars in the field, we came to the conclusion that no single definition of economic development can satisfy everyone.   Charles Kindleberger and Bruce Herrick define economic development to include "improvements in material welfare, especially for persons with the lowest incomes; the eradication of mass poverty with its correlates of illiteracy, disease, and early death; changes in the composition of inputs and outputs that generally include shifts in the underlying structure of production away from agricultural toward industrial activities."[3] Gerald Meier and Robert Baldwin, on the other hand, define economic development as a process whereby there is an increase in the real national income of an economy over a long period of time. And "if the rate of development is greater that the rate of population growth, then the per capita income will increase."[4] David Jaffee refers to socioeconomic development as "the ability to produce an adequate and growing supply of goods and services productively and efficiently, to accumulate capital, and to distribute the fruits of production in a relatively equitable manner."[5] A. H. Somjee describes development studies as being about "the problems of economic growth, political development and social change of developing societies which have come through historical and cultural experiences."[6]

We define economic development keeping in mind that an increase in well-being of the people is the desire of every individual in a society. It is a process in which there is growth in the nation's economy; where there is a sustained improvement in the well-being of the people, where there is a rise in the gross national product (GNP); where the gap between the rich and the poor decreases over time; where the decision-making process involves a greater participation of diversified groups in a society; where the entrepreneurs play a key role in the economic growth of a nation; where the private sector as opposed to the public sector, dominates the economy of the country, which has not been the case in many developing countries; and finally, a process in which government and private enterprises work hand in hand to improve the welfare of the people.

We stated earlier that economic development and economic growth can be used interchangeably. Economic growth means "more output, while economic development implies both more output and changes in the technical and institutional arrangements by which it is produced and distributed."[7] Development goes beyond this to imply "changes in the composition of output and in the allocation of inputs by sectors."[8]

Discussing the theories of economic development, Meier and Baldwin classify as economic development positive changes in factor supplies and in the structure of demand for products. Particular changes in factor supplies comprise

1. the discovery of additional resources,
2. capital accumulation,
3. population growth,
4. introduction of new and better techniques of production,
5. improvement in skills, and other institutional and organizational modification.[9]

Particular changes in the structure of demand for products are associated with development in

1. size and age composition of population,
2. level and distribution of income,
3. tastes, and
4. other institutional and organizational arrangements.[10]

This implies that economic development can be interpreted in terms of specific development in product demands and factor supplies.

Economic development is also a process where there is a sustained increase in net national product and also a rising standard of living of the population. Hence, there is an increase in both real per capita income and real national income of a nation. An increase in both real per capita income and real national income are important ingredients for the economic welfare of the population of a country. All efforts must be made between the policymakers and the public sector to see to it that the rich are not getting richer while the poor are getting poorer as is often the case in most developing countries.

Measurement of Economic Development and Democracy

There are several measures of economic development. The most common measure is the gross national product. What is gross national product? The total annual value of goods and services produced by a country is measured by the GNP. And GNP per capita means the annual value of output per individual. Hence, when there is an increase in GNP per capita over time, development has taken place. Given two points in time, the change in gross national product between these two points is called the economic growth rate. The percentage change in GNP per capita is the growth rate.

When we need to know the poverty levels in a particular country, we refer to the income distribution of that country, whereas sample surveys and censuses are used to measure unemployment and employment in a given country.

Given these measures, we can determine whether or not development is taking place in a developing country. The governments of developing countries need to set up some incentive systems to encourage development. Dennis Goulet states that "poor incentive systems necessarily generate defective development and that, conversely, sound incentive systems are the key to equitable development."[11] Goulet argues that incentive systems that are presently offered in most developing countries are biased to favor, among other things, "aggregate growth, most of the benefits of which are appropriated by privileged elite groups or classes, to the detriment of equitable growth widely shared by the neediest populace.[12] Goulet emphasizes the importance of collaboration between the elite decision-makers and the administered population over designing objective incentive systems.

A few developing countries, such as South Korea, Taiwan, Hong Kong, Singapore, Brazil, Argentina, Venezuela, Côte d'Ivoire and Senegal, have shown some encouraging economic growth in their national economies. This is due partially to government incentive systems and to privatization of the state-owned enterprises and also to the political stability in these countries. William Zartman and Christopher Delgado argue that "stability—the absence of sudden or extra-institutional shifts in leadership and policy directions, and the presence of established institutionalized processes—is important because it contributes to basic patterns of responsive government at a formative period in a new nation."[13]

Among the African countries, Côte d'Ivoire has shown, during the past twenty-five years, an annual growth rate in real terms of over 7 percent. That is a very extraordinary record to beat. To put it in the words of Bastiaan den Tuinder, "few countries, developed and developing, can match the growth rate of the Ivory Coast."[14] As we see in the subsequent chapters, privatization is well underway in Côte d'Ivoire; the government has been encouraging private enterprise in the country. It had relaxed import/export laws. The successor to the late President Houphouët-Boigny has put more emphasize on education and is surrounded by young and well-educated individuals. This is unheard of in most African countries where a minority of elites hold all the power to the detriment of the population. As a consequence most African countries were better of economically before independence than they are now, with the exception of a small ruling elite class.

Other developing countries, cited earlier, have improved the welfare of their people and have become semi-industrialized if not industrialized. The governments of these countries have opted for a free enterprise policy with emphasis on export of their manufactured goods to a point where these countries have become a real threat to the economies of the Western industrialized nations. Real authentic growth, as Goulet[15] calls it, is taking place in some of these developing countries. There is sustained economic growth, "equity in distributing the fruits of that growth, optimal procedural participation of the non-elite population in the decision-making and implementation control to development dynamics, and institutions in carrying out development activity of every sort."[16]

In most developing countries, the government, with its huge state-owned enterprises, plays the role of entrepreneur. In doing so these governments become what Raymond Duvall and John Freeman call entrepreneurial states.[17] David Jaffee states that the term entrepreneur "is usually reserved for private individuals who are innovators and risk takers, and, by virtue of these actions, stimulate economic growth and production."[18] Jaffee makes a comment that the public organization is, if anything, seen as a hindrance to this entrepreneurial process. State-owned enterprises in the developing countries, as we see in the proceeding chapters, are mismanaged. They produce goods and services that do not satisfy the demand of the consumers.

Developing countries that have departed from the strategy of import-substitution industrialization have shown an increase in their economic growth rates. Some of these developing countries are South Korea, Singapore, Hong Kong and Taiwan. Import-substitution industrialization is a development strategy that was adopted by most developing countries in the 1960s to put more emphasis on the internal production of manufactured products for domestic markets. To the contrary, the cited developing countries shifted from import-substitution industrialization to export-oriented industrialization. They are now exporting manufactured goods that compete effectively in the world market. Meanwhile, the majority of developing countries, especially those of Sub-Saharan Africa, still rely on the export of raw materials and primary products resulting in very slow, if any, economic growth. And most of them have huge balance-of-payment deficits.

What is lacking in most of these developing countries is good governmental organization. Organization plays a key role in development in two important ways: First, the rate of economic growth and the gross national product are the result of productivity and efficiency of formal work organizations. Second, "individual interests and motives are shaped by organizational forces and the resulting patterns of behavior may have significant consequences for social and political change."[19] In the late 1960s, William Hence stated that the people of the African continent face a tremendously challenging problem of improving their economic and social status from the present low levels, "which are too often characterized by poverty, ignorance, poor health, and inadequate educational facilities."[20] Today, the economic and social status of these African countries have become worse. And the Western industrialized countries have a humanitarian duty to rescue this continent, which is perishing economically.

ECONOMIC DEVELOPMENT: THEORY AND PRACTICE AND THE IMPACT OF PRIVATIZATION ON ECONOMIC DEVELOPMENT AND DEMOCRACY

Economic development has become a very important process, especially in the developing nations of the world. It is the desire of the people in those countries to improve their standard of living and to see the real national income grow. Economic development has also become a major political issue in the developing countries. Government officials are being confronted by the masses to alleviate poverty, to improve the system of education and to put in place an industrial infrastructure that would bring about sustained economic growth.

Neo-Classical Theories of Economic Development

The classical economics of Adam Smith and David Ricardo, among others, are included in this category. Smith[21] was concerned with the wealth of nations, whereas Ricardo concentrated on income distribution. Kindleberger and Herrick observe that the spirit of neo-classical models is found from "their close identification with individuals, choosing among alternatives, maximizing their own welfare in situations in which they are motivated by benefits and constrained by costs associated with any given action."[22] Smith's observations, as summarized by Diane Hunt, are that the division of labor or specialization raises the labor productivity for three reasons: "(1) workers become more efficient in the performance of particular tasks; (2) job specialization reduces time spent switching tasks; and (3) job specialization also increases the scope of designing improved tools and machines to raise labor productivity."[23]

Meier and Baldwin hold that Adam Smith attacks eighteenth-century mercantilism and argues that "nature arranges matters so that the just legal system which she prescribes is also the best means of promoting development."[24] In discussing this just legal system, which nature prescribes, Smith emphasizes the right of every individual to pursue his or her own interests free from oppression by other members. Isn't this what has to be pursued in the developing countries? For the governments to let the entrepreneurs or the private sector carry on their economic activities without any government interference, except when it is required by law. When the governments in these developing countries, especially in Sub-Saharan Africa, give total reign to individuals or to the private sector to pursue their enterprises, rapid economic growth will result that will be beneficial to the society as a whole. This is what Adam Smith meant with his famous "invisible hand" concept.

There is a need for a competitive market structure in the developing countries, and this competition can only derive from the entrepreneurs and not from the state-owned enterprises. History has proven this. Smith also put emphasis on saving, which is a necessary condition for economic development. Smith also states that once development begins, it tends to become cumulative. Division of labor will take place and the level of productivity will rise once adequate market possibilities and the basis for capital accumulation are in place.

Ricardo refines and extends the classical theory of economic development following the principles established by Adam Smith. Ricardo's argument, as summarized by Diane Hunt, is that "economic growth is financed out of the profit accruing from productive activity. If growth is to continue, it follows that the share of profits in national income must remain positive."[25] For Ricardo, agriculture is the most important sector of the economy. Ricardo identifies three major groups of actors on the economic scene in his vision of economic society: landlords, laborers and capitalists. The capitalists play a key role in the economy by directing the production of goods and services. The landlords lease their lands to the capitalists who provide tools and other means of production as well as wages, clothing and food to the workers. This is how the system is supposed to work. The state should not provide these to the people. The governments of the developing countries should not run enterprises. This task should be left to the private sector.

Extending and refining the classical theories of Adam Smith and Ricardo, neo-classical writers continue to explore the international theory of development. Heckscher and Ohlin state that each nation of the world will specialize upon the production of the commodities in which they enjoy a comparative cost advantage in real terms and export them. And they will import commodities or goods made by factors that were relatively scarce locally, resulting in a comparative cost disadvantage. In international trade both parties involved in trade ought to gain from it. Both parties should be much better off than they were before the trade began. In many developing countries, government officials in control enjoy the benefit of international trade by appropriating to themselves the gains made through the trade instead of passing it on to the rest of the population. According to neo-classical theorists, economic development is to be viewed as "a process that is generally harmonious and beneficial to all sectors of the economy."[26] There is optimism among the neo-classical theorists about the possibilities for continued economic progress. And development generally benefits all major income groups in a society. This is the view of most neo-classical economists.

Schumpeter's Analysis

J. A. Schumpeter sees a noticeable distinction between economic growth and development.[27]   In fact, he rejects the description of development stated by the neo-classical economists as a harmonious and gradual process.   Instead, Schumpeter argues that "significant advances in national product occur by disharmonious leaps and spurts as entirely new investment horizons are explored."[28]   For Schumpeter, the entrepreneur is the central figure of the development process. The entrepreneur is the innovator. Innovation may occur in the following forms: "(1) the introduction of a new good; (2) the use of a new method of production; (3) the opening of a new market; (4) the conquest of a new source of raw material supply; or (5) the reorganization of any industry."[29]   And so, for Schumpeter, the dynamics of economic development rely on the innovation of the entrepreneurs. We argue that the private sectors, with all these innovators and motivated by Smith's "invisible hand," will promote competition and efficiency and produce goods and services that meet the demands of the consumers and generate economic growth.

The crucial features of economic development, as Hunt summarizes, are not the mobilization of savings by capitalists in order to finance the accumulation of more productive capital, but "the actions of entrepreneurs in mobilizing credit to finance the procurement of existing factors of production in order to combine them in new ways." [30]

Keynesian Analysis

The major contribution of John Maynard Keynes to economic development theory is his theory on the causes of, and policy solution to, unemployment. He also contributed to the reform of international economic institutions implemented in the 1940s.   Hence, the conventional wisdom of development studies, "established in the immediate post-war period, is, in its initial presentation, quite clearly Keynesian."[31]   Keynes assumed the following elements as given and constant: "the existing skill and quantity of available labor, the existing quality and quantity of available equipment, the existing technique, the degree of competition, the tastes and habits of the consumer."[32]

The advocates of Keynesian economic theory see state intervention "as a means to prevent economic crisis and promote sustained economic depression."[33]   One of the central problems of a capitalist economy, according to Keynes, was the tendency of periodic bouts of unemployment and recession. Keynes strongly believed that these economic problems were a result of the investment behavior of capitalist firms under conditions of insufficient aggregate demand for goods and services.[34]   The logic of Keynesian theory dictates a solution that involves "progressive taxation, the redistribution of income, the expansion of social welfare programs, support for labor organization, collective bargaining, and higher wages."[35]   Higher wages to workers served to stimulate aggregate demand and mass buying power as the costs of production increased.

Structuralist theorists have adopted the economic model of John Maynard Keynes in which unemployment might persist.[36]   Structural theories focus on the composition of the economy, mainly on the sources of production.

In the field of economic development, the level and expansion of per capita income have always been the central focus of growth and development studies. As a matter of fact, Allen Kelly, Jeffrey Williamson and Russell Cheetham observe that "both in terms of the urgency of the development problem—the widening disparity of rich and poor lands—and in terms of national planning objectives, a sustained expansion in per capita consumption of the impoverished third world has been taken as one of the paramount social goals of our time."[37] Growth and development are widely viewed as a rise in per capita income.

Can economic development take place in a nation without democracy and vice versa? We are about to explore this issue of democracy in the following pages.

DEMOCRACY: THEORY AND PRACTICE

Introduction

For the past several years, many developing countries have witnessed authoritarian regimes that are being challenged by individuals and political parties.   Throughout Africa, for instance, people are fighting for "open and democratic governance, characterized by popular participation, competitive elections, and free flow of information."[38]

This trend toward democratization in the developing countries is a result of both internal and external pressures exerted on the ruling elites.   The United States and other donor nations "have elevated the funding of democratization and good governance programs to a higher priority."[39]   Within the developing countries, people have been asking government officials to deliver on their promises of economic growth and prosperity that they have been making over the years. The Western countries are pressing for democracy in the developing countries for several reasons.   Not the least of these is the fact that "democratic countries are more stable and reliable business partners than authoritarian regimes."[40] If privatization is to succeed in the developing countries, foreign investors ought to participate in this process since they have the buying power.

That means agreements will have to be signed between government officials from developing countries and foreign investors. Foreign investors would be more at ease when dealing with democratic governments than authoritarian regimes. National and foreign investors participate a great deal in the economies of countries that have democratic governments.   All these factors "translate into a better climate for foreign investment and trade."[41]

David Shinn and Timothy McCoy did a study on democratization and governance in Africa based on discussions with more than 50 practitioners and experts and a reading of vast quantities of recent literature on the subject. In making a direct causal link between democracy and sustained economic development, they argue that "democratic institutions and values can be highly supportive of efforts to address development issues and establish the basis for sustained economic growth."[42] They continue by stating that "democracy increases participation in the policy process, thus improving fairness in confronting economic hardship."[43]

I have given seminars on privatization on a number of occasions and at the same time conducted discussions on the subject with government officials in charge of privatization programs from Mali, Cameroon, Gabon, Zaire, Kenya, Tanzania, Mauritius, Morocco, Tunisia, Algeria and Brazil. I also personally visited some of these countries. Based on field research, discussions with practitioners and experts in the field and the vast quantities of recent literature reviewed and my case study, I have concluded that there is a direct causal link between privatization and economic development and democracy in the developing countries. This view is discussed throughout this study.

Talking about democracy, international statesmen gathered at Stockholm Initiative on Global Security and Governance held in April 1991 agreed that certain democratic requisites are crucial to sustain development. Necessary parts of the concept are "respect to human rights; constitutional government and the rule of the law; transparency in the wielding of power, and the accountability of those who exercise power."[44] Although the Secretary General of the Organization of African Unity (OAU), Dr. Salim A. Salim, stated at the twenty-sixth OAU summit in 1990 that democracy must be home grown, the international statesmen involved in the Stockholm Conference held in 1991 concluded that there is nevertheless "a duty for the international community to support the respect for human rights and the development of democracy. Human solidarity demands it."[45]

Although the nature and circumstances vary from one country to another, Kpundeh states that two basic patterns in the modes of transition to democracy were identified. Transitions from above take place when the ruling elites initiate democratic reforms as a result of political or mass riots. Transitions from below occur when "there are mounting popular pressures from the people resulting in national conferences, popular revolutions, coup d'etat, or pact formation, all with the goal of moving toward a more democratic society."[46] According to some scholars, democracy will be easily achieved through transitions from above, if they are well planned and well organized. Transitions from below are said to be plagued with a great deal of uncertainty.[47]

A genuine democracy requires the participation of the masses and ruling elites have to be willing to work with the masses and listen to their demands and concerns. In a democratic society such as the United States, the will of the majority of the people usually prevails in the choice of policies by the government and its decision-making process. Democracy has become the true way of life for the American people. Representatives are responsible to the voters who elect them.

What Does Democracy Mean?

A democratic society is a society that strives to observe and apply the following concepts: an elected and constitutional government, respect for human rights, participation of the masses in decisions involving their lives and respect of rules and laws. We define a democratic government as a government that respects these concepts. A democratic country should have a multi-party system, an independent judiciary, a free press and freedom of speech for its people. In a democratic society, people are to lead free and secure lives.

Several developing countries are moving toward democracy. In Africa, the democratic movement started in Benin during 1989–90, followed by Namibia's independence and elections in 1990. Encouraging signs are coming out of South Africa with a good prospect of meaningful political reforms. Democracy is thriving in South America. Chile was the last country ruled by military dictatorship, but in 1991 it transferred power to a civilian government. In Central America, only Cuba still remains under authoritarian rule, whereas democracy has been restored in Nicaragua and Panama.

What are the chances for democracy to survive in the developing countries? There have been some discouraging events that have threatened its survival there. In Togo, democracy is being tested by a former military ruler who wants to return to power by all means. In Haiti, the elected popular president was deposed. In Peru, the president with the backing of the army did away with the constitution and at the same time dismissed the elected congress. In Zaire, President Mobutu refuses any democratic reforms and holds onto power. In spite of the obstacles, democratic governments will succeed in the developing countries. The people will no longer tolerate political authoritarianism.

One definition familiar to everyone and that has become a slogan, as stated earlier, is that democracy is government of the people, by the people, for the people. In a responsive society such as democracy, no individual is excluded from the decision-making process. Keith Graham makes a distinction between direct democracy and representative democracy. In a direct democracy "the people rule by making decisions themselves, in representative democracy they elect a number of representatives to make decisions for them."[48]

Michael Margolis states that "a democracy is a polity in which democratic politics is the only politics."[49] In a democratic society, every citizen should have an equal chance to influence government policy. John Dewey argued that democracy is much broader than "a special political form, a method of conducting government, of making laws and carrying on governmental administration by means of popular suffrage and elected officials."[50] Dewey concludes that the "political and governmental phase of democracy is a means, the best means so far found, for realizing ends that lie in the wide domain of human relationships and the development of human personality."[51] For Schumpeter, democracy is "that institutional arrangement at political decisions in which individuals acquire power to decide by means of a competitive struggle for the people's vote."[52] In Margolis' view, Schumpeter's definition of democracy gives more power to the elites. He pointed out that this conception of democracy involves "the free choice of the leaders to do the governing, not the free participation of citizens in the policy-making process."[53] Hence, he concludes that the outcome of a democracy in a society depends by and large upon the quality of its leadership, not upon the rationality of its ordinary citizens.

There must be some degree of participation in any democratic system. Even a dictator, Schumpeter points out, has to enlist the cooperation of some people, while neutralizing the efforts of others.[54]

Our contention is that privatization will bring about economic development and democracy. There has to be redistribution of economic power through privatization where nationals can freely participate in purchasing shares of the newly privatized state-owned enterprises. As citizens participate freely in this process, democratic institutions will be strengthened and people will have a say in the way the country's business affairs are conducted. Nationals, as shareholders, will be able to express their preference by electing the directors of the board of these enterprises. Thus, privatization, if well carried out, will establish a democratic system where individuals have a voice in the way these newly privatized enterprises are managed and run.

Full participation by the people is the most important characteristic of a democracy. In every society, however, elites assume the leadership of the government, and these elites must be trusted by the masses.

The Economics of Democracy

We start this section by asking ourselves the same question that Howard Kainz asked, that is, Is there any necessary relationship between democracy and capitalism? Kainz states that "what we call democracy in the Anglo-American and European sense, has developed as a matter of fact in a milieu of capitalistic economic structure."[55]

Developing countries have become more tightly linked to the world economy. Africa, for instance, has become more tightly linked to the world economy for many reasons, among them the existence of "an extreme dependence on external public actors particularly IMF and the World Bank in the determination of Africa economic policy."[56] These international financial institutions along with international donors have been exerting pressure for the developing countries to privatize their state-owned enterprises. Unfortunately in many African countries, the International Monetary Fund (IMF) and the World Bank arrived too late. The state treasury "had already been privatized by the elites."[57]

There also has developed a link between aid given to a developing country and democratization and good governance. The U.S. Agency for International Development, for instance, is now "allocating its development assistance to Africa on the basis of four criteria, one of which is linked to democratization and good governance."[58]

Democracy is taking root in some developing countries that have followed the path of privatization such as Botswana, the Gambia, Mauritius, Cameroon, Senegal, Argentina, Venezuela, Brazil, Singapore, Taiwan and South Korea.

International donors strongly agree that democracy or political reforms in Africa as well as in other developing countries will take place when corruption is brought under control and ruling elites are held accountable for their handling of the nation's finances. The following must be respected: "human rights, independent media and an independent judiciary, participatory politics, and a liberalized market economy in order to move closer to the ultimate goal of meaningful economic growth and development."[59]

In order to liberalize the market economy, the government has to be willing to implement the liberalization or deregulation form of privatization that was discussed in Chapter 1. In several developing countries, it is hard or almost impossible to reduce corruption and pursue a reform of financial accountability unless the government officials hand over the management of state-owned enterprises to the private sector by either adopting the forms of privatization called management privatization or contracting out.

Privatizing state-owned enterprises would result in reduced corruption and more financial accountability and hence move closer toward the goal of meaningful economic development and democracy in a society. In any society, "holding citizens responsible for their actions, in public service and private sector, is significant to ensure level of accountability."[60]

In order for the developing countries to succeed in the privatization process that will bring about economic development and democracy, appropriate institutions based on democratic values must be established.

There is an interrelationship between democratization and economic development, as has been argued earlier. The State Department hosted a conference in 1990 in the prospect for democracy in Africa. The participants declared that "democracy and development based on free markets go together."[61] Here again we see the importance of privatization in the developing countries. In order to bring about market economy, the developing countries must privatize the state-owned enterprises.

The participants of the 1990 State Department conference also noted that "all functioning democracies in Africa and elsewhere in the world have had a significant degree of capital ownership of the means of production. Economic growth can strengthen the legitimacy of democratic institutions."[62]

We will argue that there is a definite relationship between capitalism and democracy. The Western industrialized nations that hold economic power in the world have the largest and most committed democratic systems. The group of seven industrialized nations, the United States, Canada, United Kingdom, France, Italy, Germany and Japan, each have a strong democratic system. The former Soviet Union did not have a democratic system and it was not an economic power either. The semi-industrialized nations in the developing world, South Korea, Singapore, Hong Kong, Taiwan and Brazil, have, in their own nature, some kind of democratic system. They have also established some democratic principles in their institutions.

Too many dictators in the developing countries are running their governments by dissolving democratic institutions such as the parliament, putting aside the nations' constitution and judicial system and ruling by decree.

This is definitely a false start.[63] This is what recently happened in Peru. On April 5, 1992, President Alberto Fujimori shut down Congress and suspended the constitution. Fujimori said he never intended to create a dictatorship. He stated: "We are not destroying democracy, but cleaning the ground to build a new, more efficient democracy."[64] This type of takeover happens all the time in the developing countries of Africa, Asia and Latin America.

The spirit of free enterprise in Western industrialized nations has helped to establish democratic principles in their institutions. Adam Smith's invisible hand is at work in these nations. Smith clearly sees capitalism as an adjunct to good life and human freedom. Here again, we see a positive relationship between free enterprise, privatization, democracy and economic growth.

The governments of the developing nations have to adopt the attitude of laissez-faire. This will bring about competition among private enterprises. The state-owned enterprises, which are still overrepresented in the economy have often proven to be inefficient and unproductive, and in most cases produce goods and services that are undesirable to the consumers due to their poor quality. Government intervention must cease. This would encourage individuals to run their enterprises, hence, reaching toward the goal of capitalism based on free enterprise principles. But before this can happen, government leaders have to abide by the principles of democracy. John Kenneth Galbraith makes an observation of the kind of government intervention that will prove effective in controlling and facilitating competition. He cites an example of the multinational corporations with their technostructure.[65] Kainz observes that "one thing seems certain amidst these complexities: the cause of freedom is threatened both by the power of economic organizations in the private sector and by the intervention of government."[66]

We agree with Harry Girvetz who states that "any effort to discuss democracy meaningfully without reference to economic power and the arrangements and practices through which such power is exercised and limited must be sterile."[67] As we observe the economic powers of the world, that is, the developed industrialized nations and the semi-industrialized countries, we become fully convinced that free enterprise has been the key element of capitalism and also results in a close relationship between capitalism and democracy.

The developing countries, in order to achieve this, have to proceed to the privatization of state-owned enterprises; a subject that we will discuss in Chapter 4.

However, in order to privatize, most of the developing countries, which lack economic and financial infrastructures and the know-how to privatize, need help and assistance from the Western financial institutions such as the World Bank and the International Monetary Fund as well as from Western countries such as the United States. What role, if any, has the World Bank, the International Monetary Fund and the United States played in privatization in the developing countries? We discuss this in Chapter 3.

NOTES

1 . A. H. Somjee, *Development Theory: Critiques and Explorations* (New York: St. Martin's Press, 1991), 3–15.

2. David Jaffee, *Level of Socio-Economic Development Theory* (New York: Praeger 1990), 15–49.

3. Charles P. Kindleberger and Bruce Herrick, *Economic Development* (McGraw-Hill Book Company, 1977), 1.

4. Gerald M. Meier and Robert E. Baldwin, *Economic Development Theory, History, Policy* (New York: John Wiley & Sons, Inc., 1957), 2.

5. Jaffee, *Level of Socio-Economic Development Theory,* 3.

6. Somjee, *Development Theory: Critiques and Explorations,* ix..

7. Kindleberger and Herrick, *Economic Development,* 3.

8. Ibid.

9. Meier and Baldwin, *Economic Development Theory, History, Policy,* 2.

10. Ibid., 3.

11. Dennis Goulet, *Incentives for Development: The Key to Equity* (New York: New Horizon Press, 1989), 5.

12. Ibid., 6.

13. William Zartman and Christopher Delgado, eds., *The Political Economy of Ivory Coast* (New York: Praeger Publishers, 1984), 2.

14. Bastiaan A. den Tuinder, *Ivory Coast, The Challenge of Success* (Baltimore: John Hopkins University Press, 1978), 3.

15. Dennis Goulet, *The Cruel Choice: A New Concept in the Theory of Development* (New York: Atheneum, 1971), 235ff.

16. Dennis Goulet, *Mexico: Development Strategies for the Future* (Notre Dame, Indiana: University of Notre Dame Press, 1983), 9ff.

17. Raymond Duvall and John A. Freeman, "The State and Dependent Capitalism," *International Studies Quarterly* 25 (1981): 25–105.

18. Jaffee, *Level of Socio-Economic Development Theory,* 125.

19. Ibid., 45.

20. William A. Hance, *African Economic Development* (New York: Frederick A. Praeger, 1967), 1.

21. Adam Smith, *An Inquiry into the Nature and Causes of the Wealth of Nations* (New York: The Modern Library, Random House, 1937).

22. Kindleberger and Herrick, *Economic Development,* 180.

23. Diane Hunt, *Economic Theory of Development* (Savage, Md.: Barnes & Noble Books, 1989), 10.

24. Meier and Baldwin, *Economic Development, Theory, History Policy,* 21.

25. Hunt, *Economic Theory of Development,* 14.

26. Meier and Baldwin, *Economic Development Theory, History, Policy,* 83.

27. J. A. Schumpeter, *The Theory of Economic Development* (Cambridge, Mass.: Harvard University Press, 1934), 86.

28. Ibid.

29. Ibid., 87.

30. Hunt, *Economic Theory of Development*, 25.

31. P. W. Priston, *New Trends in Development Theory: Essays in Development and Social Theory* (London: Routledge & Kegan Paul, 1985), 13.

32. John Maynard Keynes, *The General Theory of Employment Interest and Money* (New York: Harcourt, Brace and Co., 1936), 24, 245.

33. Jaffee, *Level of Socio-Economic Development Theory*, 121.

34. Robert Sidelsky, " The Decline of Keynesian Politics," in *State and Economy in Contemporary Capitalism*, ed. Colin Crouch (London: Croom Helm, 1979), 55-86.

35. Ibid., 55–56.

36. A. O. Herschman, *The Strategy of Economic Development* (New Haven, Conn.: Yale University Press, 1958).

37. Allen C. Kelley, Jeffrey G. Williamson, and Russell J. Cheetham, *Dualistic Economic Development. Theory and History* (Chicago: The University of Chicago Press, 1972), 1.

38. Sahr John Kpundeh, ed., *Democratization in Africa: Africa View, Africa Voices* (Washington, D.C.: National Research Council, Academy Press, 1992), 3.

39. David H. Shinn and Timothy S. McCoy, *Democratization and Good Governance in Africa* (Washington, D.C.: Center for Study of Foreign Affairs, Foreign Service Institute, U.S. Department of State, May 1992), v.

40. Ibid., 2.

41. Ibid.

42. Ibid.

43. Ibid.

44. Kpundeh, *Democratization in Africa: Africa View, Africa Voices*, 4.

45. Ibid.

46. Ibid., 14.

47. Ibid.

48. Keith Graham, *The Battle of Democracy: Conflict, Consensus and the Individuals* (Totowa, N. J.: Barnes & Noble Book, 1986), 16.

49. Michael Margolis, *Viable Democracy* (New York: St. Martin's Press, 1979), 22.

50. John Dewey, "Democracy is a Way of Life," in *Frontiers of Democratic Theory*, ed. Henry S. Kariel (New York: Random House, 1970), 13.

51. Ibid.

52. J. Schumpeter, *Capitalism, Socialism and Democracy*, 4th *ed.*. (London: Unwin, 1954), 269.

53. Margolis, *Viable Democracy*, 108.

54. Schumpeter, *Capitalism, Socialism and Democracy*, 245.

55. Howard P. Kainz, *Democracy East and West: A Philosophical Overview* (New York: St. Martin's Press, 1984), 80.

56. John W. Harberson and Donald Rothchild, eds., *Africa in World Politics* (Boulder, Colo.: Westview Press, 1991), 42.

57. George B. N. Ayittey, "How Africa Ruined Itself," *The Wall Street Journal*, 9 December 1992, p.1.

58. Shinn and McCoy, *Democratization and Good Governance in Africa*, v.

59. Kpundeh, ed., *Democratization in Africa: Africa View, Africa Voices*, 32.

60. Ibid., 36.

61. Shinn and McCoy, *Democratization and Good Governance in Africa*, 11.

62. Ibid., 12.

63. See René Dumond, *False Start in Africa* (New York: Frederick A. Praeger, 1966).

64. "Peru's Leader Sets Dates For Return to Democracy," *Washington Post* 22 April 1992, A 23.

65. John Kenneth Galbraith, *The New Industrial State* (New York: Signet, Penguin, 1968), 109–127.

66. Kainz, *Democracy East and West,* 85.

67. Harry K. Girvetz, *Democracy and Elitism: Two Essays with Selected Readings* (New York: Charles Scribner's Sons, 1967), 18.

3

The Role of the World Bank, International Monetary Fund and the United States in Privatization in Developing Countries

INTRODUCTION

In this chapter we explore the role that the international financial institutions, such as the World Bank, the International Monetary Fund (IMF) and the developed industrialized countries, play in the privatization process in the developing countries. Have these international financial institutions exerted pressure on the developed countries to privatize? Or are these international institutions and the United States engaged in privatization crusades in the developing nations of the world? If so, in what way? Is privatization advantageous or disadvantageous to the developing countries? And, what do international aid donors and the United States gain from the privatization process? We address these questions in this chapter.

THE WORLD BANK AND THE IMF: WHAT THEY DO, HOW THEY DO IT AND WHY THEY DO IT

Before we go any farther, we want to provide an overview of the World Bank and the IMF, two international financial institutions. What do they do, how they do it and why do they do what they do?

How did these institutions start? In July 1944, delegates from forty-four countries met in Bretton Woods, New Hampshire, and founded the International Bank for Reconstruction and Development (known as the World Bank) and the International Monetary Fund. These two institutions support the member countries' financial and economic structures on an international level. As of today, there are 156 member nations in these two financial institutions. With the breakdown of the former Soviet Union, this number will increase, because most if not all of the republics of the former Soviet Union will become members of both organizations. Both institutions are headquartered in Washington, D.C. Their main purpose is to support and strengthen the economic structures of their member nations.   One thing that needs to be clarified is that these two institutions differ.

The primary responsibility of the World Bank, when it was founded, was to finance the economic development of its member nations. Formed during the Second World War, it was given the mission to reconstruct the Western European countries ravaged by the war. It did not begin funding the developing nations until the economics of the Western European nations were strengthened and reestablished. Since the 1940s the World Bank has loaned about $210 billion to the developing countries of the world.[1]

The single central purpose of the World Bank in these developing nations is"to promote economic and social progress in developing countries by helping to raise productivity so that their people may live a better and fuller life."[2]   Where do these funds come from? Funds come through contributions by the member nations who have equity shares in the World Bank. As of 1991, the total amount of these funds was valued at approximately $175 billion.   Within the World Bank, there are two institutions, the International Bank for Reconstruction and Development (IBRD) and the International Development Association (IDA). In addition, the International Finance Corporation (IFC) is associated with the World Bank, with the task of funding private enterprises in the developing countries. Also associated with the World Bank are the International Center for Settlement of Investment Disputes and the Multilateral Guarantee Agency. Over 6,000 staff members work for the World Bank and its affiliate financial institutions in well over forty offices around the world. Only 5 percent of its staff work outside its Washington, D.C., offices. These staff members are from a variety of educational backgrounds, not only economists.

The IMF has a staff of about 2,000 members. Almost all of them work in Washington, D.C., with the exception of a handful who work in New York, Paris and Geneva. And unlike the staff of the World Bank, the staff members of the IMF are constituted mainly of experts in finance and economics. All members of the IMF are required to sign a code of conduct. According to the code, member nations are required to allow their currency to be exchanged for foreign currencies freely and without restriction. The code also stipulates that members keep the IMF informed of changes they contemplate on financial and monetary policies that will affect the economies of other members. Members are strongly encouraged to "modify these policies on the advice of the IMF to accommodate the needs of the entire membership."[3]

There are a number of governments in the developing countries that have repeatedly refused to adhere to this code of conduct, especially those in Africa. Most are now in deep financial trouble, with inflation galloping over 4,000 percent in certain Sub-Saharan African countries. For example, in Zaire the inflation rate reached an astonishing 300,000 percent a year in 1992, according to the State Department.[4]   These governments view the IMF as a political institution trying to dictate the economic policies of their sovereign states. According to the IMF, it does not impose any decision on its 156 member nations, maintaining that it "has no effective authority over the internal economic policies of its members."[5] The IMF oversees the international monetary system and although it is not a lending institution such as the World Bank, the IMF gives loans to its members to support the system. For instance, from 1983 to 1984, "the IMF lent some $28 billion to member countries having difficulty meeting their financial obligations to other members."[6] But the primary purpose of the IMF remains that of helping formulate better economic policies of its member countries.

The IMF source of finance is through membership fees or quota subscriptions. These quotas were worth about $130 billion as of January 1992. Although 75 percent of quotas is paid in domestic money by its members, the IMF has many members from the developing countries that cannot afford to pay the remaining 25 percent in hard currency. The major convertible currencies used by borrowers from the IMF are the U.S. dollar, the deutsche mark, the French franc, the pound sterling and the Japanese yen. The line of credit to borrowers now amounts to $25 billion. The members have the right to borrow from the IMF over and above the amount they paid in as a quota subscription. Many developing countries, especially in Africa, cannot pay their debts, and interest on debts has been skyrocketing. This is a prevalent problem not only in Sub-Saharan Africa but also in the developing countries of Latin America. Consequently, many of these developing countries have defaulted on their loan payments. At the present time the borrower pays in service charges and commitment fees "about 1/2 of 1 percent of the amount borrowed and in interest charges about 9 percent."[7]

The IMF has a mechanism termed a stand-by arrangement, which provides a line of credit for up to three years to any member that is experiencing some kind of difficulty in staying current in its foreign obligations. This mechanism is being widely used in the developing nations of Africa, Asia and Latin America and is being funded by IMF members of the developed industrialized nations. The fund to finance this stand-by arrangement is valued at $12 billion. The interest rate charged for this mechanism is much less than that previously discussed.

The IMF, in addition to its main purpose of supervising international monetary systems and providing financial support to its members, runs an educational institute in Washington that trains employees from central banks and finance ministries of its member countries.

Since the breakdown of the Soviet empire, the IMF has tackled another mission, that of assisting the countries of Eastern Europe to implement market economies. It is providing funds and expertise to help build these new economic and financial structures. In 1985 the World Bank and the IMF began assisting developing countries of Asia, Africa and Latin America with improvements to their economic infrastructure in order to eliminate mismanagement, which has slowed and in some cases eliminated economic growth in these countries. This is known as the structural adjustment program with a fund valued at $12 billion financed by members of the developed industrialized countries.

In order to respond to the financial crisis in the poorer developing countries, the International Monetary Fund has equipped itself with two new facilities: the structural adjustment facility (SAF) in March 1986 and the enhanced structural adjustment facility (ESAF) in December 1987. These two facilities, with a fund valued at SDR 8.7 (about US$12) billion,[8] serve the main purpose of helping the poorer developing countries with protracted payment problems take measures to improve their balance of payments and to foster economic growth.

The structural adjustment facility and the enhanced structural adjustment facility establish a procedure "to build consensus on an adjustment program within the borrowing country and among the international lending and donor communities and they provide a rallying point for the mobilization of additional funds."[9]   These two facilities have been of great help to these low-income countries where prices for exports have been falling over the years and their external debts increasing.

Altogether, the sixty-one poorest members of the International Monetary Fund were eligible to use the SAF and the ESAF. The eligible members can receive up to 250 percent of quota under ESAF over a three-year program period, with provisions for up to 350 percent in some exceptional circumstances.

Table 3.1 shows that by the end of February 1991, thirty-two low-income developing countries have obtained support from SAF. And Table 3.2 shows fourteen low-income nations that had obtained support from the ESAF for their structural adjustment programs. These programs are developed by the member country, with the help of the staffs of the IMF and the World Bank. Their aim is to establish conditions in these countries in order to achieve higher rates of economic growth.

We suggest that the developing countries, with the blessings of the World Bank and the IMF, use a portion of these funds provided by the adjustment facility and the enhanced structural adjustment facility to invest in the privatization process. Since privatization has a positive impact on economic development and democracy, a portion of these funds would enhance the privatization process. And privatization will also foster economic growth, which is also the objective of the two structural adjustment facilities.

In the following section we explore the role that the United States, the World Bank and the International Monetary Fund play in privatization in the developing countries.   Did they exert any pressure on these developing countries to privatize?

Table 3.1
Structural Adjustment Facility (SAF) and Enhanced Structural Adjustment Facility (ESAF)   Arrangements as of End of February 1991
(in millions of SDRs)

Member	Date of Agreement	Amount Committed	Amount Disbursed
SAF Arrangements			
Bangladesh	February 6, 1987	201.25	201.25
Benin	June 16, 1989	21.91	6.26
Bolivia	December 15, 1986	63.49	18.14
Burundi	August 8, 1986	29.89	29.89
Central African Rep.	June 1, 1987	21.28	21.28
Chad	October 30, 1987	21.42	21.42
Dominica	November 26, 1986	2.80	2.80
Equatorial Guinea	December 7, 1988	12.88	3.68
Gambia	September 17, 1986	11.97	8.55
Ghana	November 6, 1987	143.15	40.90
Guinea	July 29, 1987	40.53	28.95
Guinea-Bissau	October 14, 1987	5.25	3.75
Haiti	December 17, 1986	30.87	8.82
Kenya	February 1, 1988	99.40	28.40
Lao People	September 18, 1989	20.51	5.86
Dem. Rep. Guinea	—	—	—
Lesotho	June 29, 1988	10.57	10.57
Madagascar	August 31, 1987	46.48	13.28
Mali	August 5, 1988	35.56	25.40
Mauritania	September 22, 1986	23.73	16.95
Mozambique	June 8, 1987	42.70	42.70
Nepal	October 14, 1987	26.11	26.11
Niger	November 17, 1986	23.59	16.85
Pakistan	December 28, 1988	382.41	273.15
Sao Tome & Principe	June 2, 1989	2.80	0.80
Senegal	November 10, 1986	59.57	42.55
Sierra Leone	November 14, 1986	40.53	11.58
Somalia	June 29, 1987	30.94	8.84
Sri Lanka	March 9, 1988	156.17	156.17
Tanzania	October 30, 1987	74.90	74.90
Togo	March 16, 1988	26.88	7.68
Uganda	June 15, 1987	69.72	49.80
Zaire	May 15, 1987	203.70	145.50
Total		**1,982.96**	**1,352.78**

Source: Joslin Landell-M *Helping the Poor: the IMF's New Facilities for Structural Adjustment* (Washington, D.C.: International Monetary Fund, 1991), 6.

Table 3.2
Members - Date of Agreement - Amount Committed - Amount Disbursed

Member	Date of Agreement	Amount Committed	Amount Disbursed
ESAF Arrangements			
Bangladesh	August 10, 1990	258.75	43.13
Bolivia	July 27, 1988	136.05	90.70
The Gambia	November 23, 1988	20.52	17.10
Ghana	November 9, 1988	368.10	272.10
Guyana	July 13, 1990	81.52	37.24
Kenya	May 15, 1989	241.40	180.93
Madagascar	May 15, 1989	76.90	51.27
Malawi	July 15, 1988	55.80	55.80
Mauritania	May 24, 1989	50.85	16.95
Mozambique	June 1, 1990	85.40	9.15
Niger	December 12, 1988	50.55	23.59
Senegal	November 21, 1988	144.67	102.12
Togo	May 31, 1989	46.08	30.72
Uganda	April 17, 1989	179.28	102.09
Total		1,795.87	1,032.89
Total SAF and ESAF Arrangements		3,778.83	2,385.67

Source: Joslin Landell-Mills, *Helping the Poor: The IMF's New Facilities for Structural Adjustment* (Washington, D.C.: International Monetary Fund, 1991), 7.

U.S. POLICY TOWARD PRIVATIZATION IN THE DEVELOPING COUNTRIES

Because of the debt crisis in the developing countries, several Western governments, including the United States, especially during the Reagan Administration, have supported privatization in the developing countries. Developed industrialized countries see privatization as the best way to promote sustained economic growth in the developing countries. The multinational corporations that have operations in the developing countries have also supported increased privatization in these countries.

Does the United States have a policy toward privatization in the developing countries? And, if so what is it? In a memorandum dated April 1985, Assistant Secretary of Treasury, David Mulford, stated that the United States should "support private sector-oriented growth, encourage privatization, and discourage, where appropriate, direct government activity in the economy."[10] The United States, therefore, has since adopted a policy that supports privatization in the developing economies. The U.S. Agency for International Development (USAID), for instance, is the best American vehicle for promoting privatization projects in the developing countries. The Federal Reserve Board has also promoted privatization by using an amendment to its Regulation K, which had limited to 20 percent the ownership an American commercial bank can have in a nonfinancial enterprise. A commercial bank is allowed to acquire up to 100 percent of such an entity under the following conditions:

1. the nonfinancial firm must be in the process of being transferred from public to private ownership;
2. the country in which the company is located must be heavily indebted;
3. the shares must be acquired through a debt-equity swap.[11]

THE WORLD BANK AND IMF POLICY TOWARD PRIVATIZATION

Have the World Bank and the IMF been exerting pressure on the developing countries to privatize their large public sectors? Some scholars have argued that these two international financial institutions have supported privatization in the developing countries, whereas others have denied that these institutions have exerted pressure on these countries.

The World Bank's lending programs have shown some measures designed to improve performance of the state-owned enterprises. Between 1980 and 1986 forty structural adjustment loans were introduced in twenty-one developing countries. Out of these 73 percent called for some action in the financial performance of the public enterprise. Paul Mosley found that 62 percent of the programs called for deregulation of pricing or licensing legislation as a requirement.[12] A detailed examination of the programs shows that "the emphasis in the Bank's recommendations has been on the deregulation and competition rather than on divestiture."[13] However, Mosley states that in particular, it has been widely suggested that "the Bank is trying to resolve the problem by widespread programs of privatization of state-owned enterprise in the developing countries."[14] The World Bank and other institutions believed that poverty and financial crisis in the developing countries were a result of the economic policies adopted over the years by the governments of these countries. The state-owned enterprises have become too large and inefficient. These public enterprises make no profits due to mismanagement, the large number of civil servants employed in the public sector which drain government revenue and the fact that all of the decisions in the public sector are made by political appointees who in most cases lack knowledge in the field.

Cook and Kirkpatrick state that bilateral agencies such as USAID and international financial institutions, particularly the World Bank and the IMF, have exerted pressure on developing countries to undergo privatization.[15] However, many governments in the developing countries have been reluctant to fully commit themselves to the idea of privatization. Since many of them do not understand the privatization process and its implications, policymakers in the developing countries have undertaken privatization measures primarily to ensure the continued inflow of foreign aid from international lending institutions and international donors. It has been proven that privatization is hard to achieve in some countries and that there have been some failures; but overall privatization would help improve the economic growth of the developing countries.

The World Bank and the IMF put pressure on the developing countries that were experiencing severe financial crises in the 1970s to reduce the role of the state in the public enterprises and to sell these public enterprises that were operating at a loss to the private sector.[16]

In pressing for privatization in the developing countries, there may be some debate as to who should be the buyers. In some poorer developing countries the potential buyers may wind up being multinational corporations and not nationals. Since the ownership of multinational corporations is primarily based in the Western world, the inequalities in the distribution of wealth between the developed and developing countries will widen. Hence, many governments in the developing countries have refused to sell national assets to foreign owners. This would be a return to colonialism, they argue. The World Bank, the IMF and the international donors are aware of this problem. These institutions are helping the developing countries with the structural adjustment loan programs. They are encouraging competition and efficiency in the developing countries to foster economic growth. The growth in the size of the public sector, especially in Sub-Saharan Africa, has increased over the years due to inefficiencies, distortions in the delivery of services and lack of competition. The programs undertaken by the World Bank and IMF will help promote economic growth in the developing countries. Since these developing countries, especially in Sub-Saharan Africa, have run out of money and credit "the chief push factors have been substantial external pressure from the IMF, the World Bank, and the international donor countries in a context of heavily direct and implied conditionality and a desperate need for external resources on the part of African governments"[17] The productivity growth in these countries has been less that satisfactory. There has been low profitability due to mismanagement and government interferences in day-to-day operations of the public enterprises, in particular from the political powers. Hence, public sectors in the developing countries have failed to generate revenue and failed to contribute to sustained economic growth.

Don Babai states that two international institutions—the World Bank and the IMF—stand out among a number of players that have exerted external stimulus toward privatization in developing countries.[18] The World Bank and the IMF have attributed instability and the lack of economic growth in most developing countries to government interventions in those countries. These two international financial institutions have been critical of the state-owned enterprises that were unable to meet their economic and social goals. These state-owned enterprises have caused budgetary burdens and huge deficits due to their mismanagement, inefficiency and the poor quality of goods and services they produce. The World Bank and the IMF favor the elimination of state-owned enterprises that "simply never should have been created in the first place"[19] This especially applies to the state-owned enterprises in Sub-Saharan Africa. The World Bank and the IMF have called for governments in the developing countries to promote private enterprises. Hence, the two institutions have put more emphasis on privatization in their lending programs in developing countries, especially in the Bank's structural adjustment loans. Have the two institutions encouraged privatization in the developing countries? The answer is a resounding yes.

The World Bank and the IMF as well as other international donors have argued that in order to promote economic growth and development in the developing countries the emphasis must be shifted from the state-owned enterprises to private enterprises. The private sector will help meet the two previously stated objectives. Hence, the principal objective of the World Bank has been to promote private investment. This is specifically stipulated in its Articles of Agreement.[20] For more than twenty year the World Bank policy has opposed any direct funding for state-owned enterprises in the developing countries. However in the 1970s, the International Finance Corporation funded projects of state-owned enterprises in the developing countries.[21] In the 1980s the World Bank reversed this policy of funding state-owned enterprises and together with the IMF started assessing those enterprises.

State-owned enterprises proved to be a heavy burden to governments in the developing countries. Short reports on a study of thirty-four developing countries, and the findings were that the average net budgetary payments to state-owned enterprises was 3.3 percent of gross domestic product (GDP) in the mid-1970s. In these thirty-four developing countries, the budgetary burdens represented three-fourth of the total deficits of the governments.[22] Don Babai states that in some African countries, "the cumulative loses of state-owned enterprises were found to exceed 5 percent of GDP in the early 1980s."[23] Based on several studies, the World Bank concluded that the state-owned enterprises are not meeting the needs of the population, they are inefficient and noncompetitive. Hence, the World Bank has embraced privatization in the developing countries. The most preferred form of privatization by the Bank was sales of assets to the private sector which the World Bank characterized as a "promising avenue" for these developing countries.[24]

The IMF has also expressed some concerns about the state-owned enterprises in the developing countries. Hence, the IMF has shown some interest in privatization in these countries. The IMF is more concerned about the balance-of-payments, fiscal and monetary policy as well as the government deficit in these developing countries.[25]

In a way, the World Bank and the IMF have embraced privatization in the developing countries as a means rather than as an end. Privatization, to both the World Bank and the IMF, remains a rationale in search of a policy, as J. A. Kay and D. J. Thompson put it.[26] The World Bank is more explicitly oriented toward the promotion of the private sector than in the past, whereas the International Monetary Fund has stabilization programs for developing countries with balance-of-payments problems that favor the export sector and push resources in the direction of the private sector. Privatization is, indeed, sweeping the world. This is a widely shared perception. The state-owned enterprises on which so much hope was placed have failed to satisfy the needs of the consumers and have become more and more of a burden, as they have drained governments budgets in most instances.

There is a connection between the data presented in this chapter and the main argument of this book. For instances, from 1983 to 1984, the IMF total loans to its member countries having difficulty meeting their financial obligations to other members amounted to $ 28 billion. Developing countries benefited from these loans. Most of these funds, in the case of developing countries, went to refinance public enterprises. These funds landed in the hands of government officials who, in most cases, diverted them to other uses. During our research, we found this to be the case in several developing countries among them, Zaire, Zambia, Côte d'Ivoire, Gabon, Chile, Peru and Indonesia. Hence, these funds, supposedly injected in public enterprises, did not have any positive impact on economic development and democracy in the developing countries.

The interests on debts alone keep increasing, and as a consequence many of the developing countries have defaulted on their loan payments.

Our recommendation is that the developing countries should use a portion of the funds provided by the adjustment facility and the enhanced structural adjustment facility to invest in the privatization process.

This chapter also asserts that public enterprises must be privatized because of their poor economic performance. Literature reviewing performance of public enterprises in several countries is readily available. Ramesh Adhikari and Colin Kirkpatrick for instances, did an empirical review of public enterprises in the developing countries.[27] Leroy Jones, Pankaj Tandon and Ingo Vogelsang also did an empirical study on public enterprise in several developing countries.[28] John Nellis also conducted an empirical study of public enterprise in Sub-Saharan Africa.[29] R. P. Short conducted an empirical study on the role of public enterprises in the developing countries.[30] All these empirical studies have delivered a critical assessment of public enterprises. They present a depressing picture of budgetary burdens, losses, inefficiency and poor product and service to consumers. And that these state-owned enterprises are incapable of meeting their economic and social goals. Nellis argues that "public enterprises simply never should have been created in the first place."[31]

Chapter 4 deals with privatization in the developing countries: theories and practice.

NOTES

1. David D. Driscoll, *The IMF and The World Bank: How Do They Differ?* (Washington, D.C.: International Monetary Fund, 1992), 2.

2. Ibid.

3. Ibid., 3.

4. Mr. Mobutu's Obligation to Zaire," *Washington Post* 6 April 1992, p. A 12.

5. David D. Driscoll, *What is the International Monetary Fund?* (Washington, D.C.: International Monetary Fund, 1992), 1.

6. Ibid., 13.

7. Ibid., 18.

8. Joslin Landell-Mills, *Helping the Poor: The IMF's New Facilities for Structural Adjustment* (Washington, D.C.: International Monetary Fund, 1991), 1.

9. Ibid.

10. Quoted in J. William Middendorf, Jr., *Implementing the Baker Initiative* Current Policy, No. 781 (Washington, D.C.: U.S. Department of State, 1986).

11. Regulation K, International Banking Operations (Washington, D.C.: Federal Reserves Press Release, August 12, 1987).

12. Paul Mosley, "Privatization Policy-Based Lending and World Bank Behaviour," in *Privatization in Less Developed Countries*, eds. Paul Cook and Colin Kirkpatrick (New York: St. Martin's Press, 1988), 125–139.

13. Cook and Kirkpatrick, *Privatization in Less Developed Countries*, 29.

14. Mosley, "Privatization Policy-Based Lending and World Bank Behaviour," 125.

15. Cook and Kirkpatrick, *Privatization in Less Developed Countries*, 30.

16. For information, see Berg Report, *Accelerated Development in Sub-Saharan Africa* (Washington, D.C.: The World Bank, 1981).

17. Thomas M. Callaghy and Ernest J. Wilson III, "Africa: Policy, Reality or Ritual?" in *The Promise of Privatization: A Challenge for U.S. Policy*, ed. Raymond Vernon (New York: Council on Foreign Relations Books, 1988), 186.

18. Don Babai, "The World Bank and the IMF: Rolling Back the State or Backing its Role?" in *The Promise of Privatization: A Challenge for U.S. Policy*, ed. Raymond Vernon (New York: Council on Foreign Relations Books, 1988), 254.

19. For more, see John R. Nellis, "Public Enterprises in Sub-Saharan Africa," World Bank Discussion paper No. 1 (Washington, D.C.: The World Bank, 1986), 32–43.

20. International Bank for Reconstruction and Development, *Articles of Agreement, Article 1 (ii) and Article III, Section 4 (ii)*.

21. International Finance Corporation, *Annual Report*, 1981, 13.

22. R. P. Short, "The Role of Public Enterprises: An International Statistical Comparison," in *Public Enterprises in Mixed Economies: Some Microeconomic Aspects*, ed. Robert H. Floyd et al. (Washington, D.C.: International Monetary Fund, 1984), 169.

23. Babai, "The World Bank and the IMF, 263.

24. *World Bank Development Report 1987* (Washington, D.C.: The World Bank, 1987), 68.

25. Vito Tanzi and Mario I. Blejer, "Fiscal Deficits and Balance of Payments Disequilibrium in IMF Adjustment Programs," in *Adjustment, Conditionality and International Financing*, ed. Joaquin Muns (Washington, D.C.: International Monetary Fund, 1984), 117–136.

26. J. A. Kay and D. J. Thompson, "Privatization: A Policy in Search of a Rationale," *Economic Journal* 96 (March 1986): 18–22.

27. Ramesh Adhikari and Colin Kirkpatrick, "Public Enterprise in Less Developing Countries: An Empirical Review," in *Public Enterprise at the Crossroads: Essays in Honour of V. V. Ramanadham,* ed. John Heath (New York: Routledge: 1990), 25–43.

28. Leroy P. Jones, Pankaj Tandon, Ingo Vogelsang, *Selling Public Enterprises: A Cost-Benefit Methodology* (Cambridge, Mass.: The MIT Press, 1990).

29. John Nellis, "Public Enterprises in Sub-Saharan Africa," World Bank Discussion Paper, No. 1 (Washington, D.C.: The World Bank, 1986), 32–43.

30. R. P. Short, "The Role of Public Enterprises: An International Statistical Comparison," in *Public Enterprise in Mixed Economies: Some Microeconomic Aspects,* eds. Robert H. Floyd el. al. (Washington, D.C.: International Monetary Fund, 1984), 169.

31. Nellis, "Public Enterprises in Sub-Saharan Africa," 32–43.

Privatization in Developing Countries: Theory and Practice

INTRODUCTION

In almost all developing countries, the public sector, largely composed of state-owned enterprises, has become too large. Governments have been running large deficits. In order to help finance these deficits in the public sector, state-owned enterprises have been borrowing heavily from central government transfers and from national and international financial markets.[1] In the 1970s, over 25 percent of state-owned enterprises' deficits were financed by direct foreign borrowing.

The prospects for economic development and democracy in Africa are much greater through privatization than through state-owned enterprises. Pressure has been "applied on developing countries by international organizations such as the World Bank, International Monetary Fund (IMF), and the U.S. Agency for International Development to pursue the policy of privatization as a part of a package of economic reforms."[2] In order for the leaders of the developing countries to see privatization as their best alternative, they have to be trained and educated in this field through seminars conducted by scholars and practitioners who have know-how in this field.

Foreign aid and foreign borrowing in the last thirty years, as we have seen, have not brought economic development and democracy because these funds are not being used for the purpose for which they were intended. This privatization is going to bring about economic development and democracy, in most cases; not repression and authoritarianism. The likelihood that privatization will result in democracy is much greater than the threat of nationalization because with less foreign aid and borrowing, people are going to look after their interests in privatized enterprises, as we see in Chapter 7.

STATE-OWNED ENTERPRISES VERSUS PRIVATE SECTOR

The public sector has been the largest employer in the developing countries. Governments of developing countries set economic, social and political goals in running state-owned enterprises. The economic objective has consisted of the public sector contributing to the process of development and economic growth. This, however, did not materialize. The developing countries have therefore expressed interest in privatization as the only alternative to help meet economic objectives of economic growth and development. The social goals of state-owned enterprises in developing countries have consisted of providing employment to the population and subsidizing industries in the production of goods and services. And lastly, the political objectives have consisted of generating power and pride for the populations who run the government in providing employment to a large number of people.

Even though the public sector failed to meet these economic, social and political goals, some government leaders in the developing countries also defended the role of the public sector as instrumental in the redistribution of income. This, however, has not proven to be the case.[3] On the contrary, the public sector has become a constraint on economic development and on the distribution of wealth and income. Furthermore, most developing countries have opted for capital-intensive technology due to the nature of their strategic industries, and this has resulted in a reduction in employment.

In spite of the ill-effects of capital-intensive technology on public sector employment, state-owned enterprises in most of the developing countries account for a great share of investment and national output. Although developing countries constitute an important part of the global economy, "accounting for 76 percent of world population, 31 percent of world trade, and experiencing rates of population growth two to three times those of the industrialized countries,"[4] the limitations placed on economic growth and development are staggering when considering government restrictions placed on the average citizen who attempts to make full use of his or her entrepreneurial spirit. It is not surprising that the informal economy has flourished under these conditions.[5] Bureaucratic red tape has contributed to the economic malaise, coupled with public sector domination of industrial output and production.

The origins of public sector growth can be traced back to the immediate post-independence period. The desire for developing countries to build industrial infrastructures based on import substitution helped to establish state-owned enterprises.[6] The developing countries inherited this public sector growth from the colonial powers, and the problem became acute during the post-independence era. This led many developing countries to consider the concept of privatization in their state-owned enterprises. Upon attaining independence in the 1950s and 1960s, developing countries in Africa and Asia inherited systems of monopoly export that were left in place by the colonizers.[7] The colonial powers built public enterprises in the developing countries because they wanted those enterprises to cover their own generated costs. The costs involved in building the little economic infrastructure that existed at that time, the cost to train and maintain public forces and the costs of the colonial governors and public servants were to come from the public sector apparatus. When these colonies became independent, they inherited this large public sector, which has become larger over the years.

It was observed in developed economies that markets in the developing countries frequently failed to work in the 1950s and 1960s. There was a need for the state to intervene and participate actively in order to offset these market failures. This led to the widespread adoption of economic planning and to an increase in the number of state-owned enterprises.[8] This is what is termed the interventionist approach, which was supported in the 1950s and 1960s by international institutions such as the World Bank and the International Monetary Fund as well as by major international aid donors which allocated funds to state-owned enterprises in the developing countries.[9]

The role of price mechanisms and markets in the development process is emphasized in the neoclassical approach. Adhikari and Kirkpatrick argue that policy prescriptions that flow from neoclassical analysis "involve the removal of various forms of government intervention in product and factor markets that are seen as distorting the price signals and repressing the market mechanism."[10] Hence, the neoclassical approach emphasizes and encourages the reduction of the size of the public sector, removal of government controls and regulation and promotion of competition. As discussed in Chapter 1, privatization may promote competition among the newly privatized firms, reduce costs and provide better quality of goods and services produced at a competitive price in the marketplace. This has been proven to be the case in the privatization of local government functions in the United States, Europe and some developing countries. The public sector has proven to be ineffective. The private sector can manage firms more effectively and deliver goods and services to the public more efficiently and at a lower cost than the public sector because of their know-how.[11] There is ample evidence that the privatization of local government functions in Great Britain, France, Italy, the United States and developing countries has unleashed a torrent of innovative creativity on the part of private entrepreneurs.[12] Yair Aharoni states that professional economists have largely accepted the idea that privatization may lead to more competition and achieve greater efficiency.[13] Thomas Callaghy and Ernest Wilson are in agreement with Yair Aharoni and Cohen that privatization can, indeed, generate extensive provision of goods and services, greater economic efficiency, "wider participation in the benefit of economic development and renewed growth that can come from improved capital formation and investment."[14]

Despite the interventionist approach and the investment support from international institutions and donor, developing countries failed to meet their goals of economic development and growth.[15] Instead, they performed very poorly in almost all the projects invested in.[16] There were widespread inefficiencies and resources misallocation in the import substitution industrialization strategy. In the 1950s and early 1960s, import substitution industrialization formed an integral part of the interventionist approach to development in developing countries.[17]   As argued earlier, these inefficiencies and poor performance in the public sector have motivated most developing countries to opt for privatization.

How has privatization worked so far in those developing countries where it has been tested? What problems has privatization encountered? And who are the buyers of newly privatized state-owned enterprises?   These questions are discussed later on in this chapter. But, for now, we raise the question, Why have the state-owned enterprises failed? There are several reasons, among them, lack of managerial skill and know-how, since most of the top staff of these firms were usually political appointees who lacked expertise in the field. This political interference has also been the most common cause of inefficiency and mismanagement of state-owned enterprises.[18]

These inefficiencies, poor performance, low quality of goods and services, misallocation of resources and lack of managerial skills have caused a budgetary burden for the state-owned enterprises. The deficit has been increasing in the developing countries. Deficit is defined as "the difference between current plus capital expenditure and revenue plus receipts of current transfers and non-government capital transfers."[19]   This growing deficit in the governments of the developing countries has been one of the motivating interests for privatization. In most developing countries, many state-owned enterprises have drained budgetary resources, contributed to overall public sector deficits, weakened fiscal management, and made a negative contribution to value added.[20]

Information on the size of public enterprises in terms of their share in total investment and value added is shown in Table 4.1. In a sample of twenty-eight developing countries in 1984–85, the GDP-weighted share in total value added in those countries was 10.9 percent, whereas in the developed countries the equivalent value added share was 8 percent on a GDP-weighted basis for the period of 1975–79.[21] John Heath argues that "because of the substantial share of public enterprise in total value added and investment, their operating performance is of major importance to the overall performance of an economy."[22]

Many scholars have concluded that the developing countries have performed poorly. How can performance evaluation be viewed? It can be viewed from two broad micro and macro perspectives. The micro-perspective of public enterprise performance focuses "on commercial profitability and financial performance, and on economic performance, usually on an annual basis."[23]   The macro-analysis of performance deals with a contribution toward the country's economy in terms of foreign exchange earnings, investment and savings and creation of employment.[24] The macro-analysis of performance also looks at other issues that are burdens to the economy of a nation in terms of foreign debts and the impact on balance-of-payment, guarantees, subsidies and deficits.[25] We would like to caution that privatization should not be taken as an answer to all the problems encountered by governments through state-owned enterprises.[26] Privatization can be a very complex issue and its implementation can raise some serious economic, social and political concerns. If privatization is not well thought through and planned, it is doomed to fail.[27]

Table 4.1

Share of Public Enterprise Sector in Total Investment and Value Added, Mid-1980s

Country	Total Investment %	Total Value Added %
Zambia (1984)	77.5	41.3
Burma (1984)	69.8	24.1
Venezuela (1984)	52.2	29.9
Guyana (1984)	41.9	22.7
India (1985)	41.1	n.a
Tunisia (1984)	38.7	24.0
Algeria (1985)	33.4	10.1
Morocco (1985)	33.1	15.4
Turkey (1985)	30.5	9.0
Congo (1985)	29.0	10.6
Tanzania (1984)	28.0	11.4
Chile (1985)	27.5	16.8
Zaire (1983)	22.8	n.a.
Bangladash (1985)	22.1	2.3
Portugal (1984)	20.4	14.6
Kenya (1984)	19.6	8.0
Mexico (1984)	19.1	13.1
Brazil (1985)	17.5	3.5
Philippines (1984)	15.3	3.7
Nepal (1984)	14.1	1.8
Costa Rica (1985)	13.2	4.3
Jamaica (1984)	11.0	21.0
Mauritius (1984)	7.2	n.a.
Dominican Republic (1984)	7.0	3.3
Developing countries (1984)*	28.2	10.9
Industrial countries (1975–9)+	9.9	8.0

Sources: Nair and Filippides (1988) as quoted in John Heath, ed.,*Public Enterprise at the Crossroads: Essays in Honour of V.V. Ramanadham* (London: Routledge, 1990), 26.

Notes: *Twenty-eight countries average for value added and thirty-seven countries average for investment. Value added weighted by GDP. For Burma and all African countries the investment averages are of public enterprise investment to gross investment, in other cases, the ration is a share of gross fixed capital formation.

+ Six Organization for Economic Cooperation and Development (OECD) countries weighted by 1977 GDP for value added, and for investment, thirteen industrial countries.

THE WHYS AND WHEREFORES OF PRIVATIZATION IN THE DEVELOPING COUNTRIES AND ITS IMPACT ON ECONOMIC DEVELOPMENT AND GROWTH

In this section we discuss and review the theories and practice of the whys and wherefore of privatization in the developing countries. All the issues we discussed in the preceding section have served as a background for the concern and interest of the governments of developing countries toward privatization.

As discussed earlier, privatization increases the quality of goods and services, leads to open and competitive economies that create more jobs, increases income and allows individuals to hold stocks in the newly privatized state-owned enterprises. Peter McPherson summarizes the issue by stating that for the purpose of liberating the economies of developing countries from the slow growth or stagnation that has plagued so many of them since independence, privatization can be the answer.[28] Privatization has indeed become a viable development and economic policy option for most of the developing countries. Governments should not be entrepreneurs and producers of goods and services. They need to delegate these functions to the private sector. Thus, privatization may be the solution to economic weaknesses and inefficiencies, poverty, mismanagement, deficits and huge government payrolls. Based on the outcome of the public enterprises for the last few decades, the developing countries should think of how to privatize and not wonder whether or not to privatize. Alan Waters comments that economic theory is "quite explicit: because of the nature of ownership and incentives, a state entity cannot be as efficient as a private entity in the production of the same output."[29]

There are a few other questions to raise concerning privatization in the developing countries: Where is adequate capital to finance privatization, who are the buyers of stocks and what are the social and political consequences of privatization?

The developing countries' interest in privatization has increased over the years through demands for assistance and advice from the U.S. Agency for International Development (USAID) offices around the world as well as through the international donors' desire to see developing countries privatize the public sectors. The World Bank and the International Monetary Fund have also exerted pressure on the developing countries to privatize their state-owned enterprises.[30]

The developing countries do not have knowledge as to how to privatize since the process of privatization is complex and very demanding. In order for privatization to succeed, developing countries need assistance in developing capital markets, reforming macro-economic policies and providing credit facilities to promote the expansion of the public sector.[31] In order for the privatization process to work in the developing nations of Asia, Africa and Latin America, the financial cooperation and collaboration of developed industrialized nations as well as that of the international financial institutions is essential. It is almost impossible for privatization to take place without sufficient capital in the private hands of potential national buyers. Significant efforts are being made in the developing nations of Asia and Southeast Asia to privatize the public sector. Financial institutions have been developed in Singapore, Hong Kong, South Korea, Indonesia, Malaysia and others. Privatization offers several choices and opportunities to developing countries.[32]

In Latin America, several countries have long been committed to privatization, particularly Mexico, Chile, Argentina, Venezuela, Brazil, Jamaica and Belize. Paul Roberts contends that free enterprise through privatization will set Latin America free.[33] All these countries have opted for privatization as a means to eradicate poverty, to increase income, to promote competition and to offer a better quality of goods and services to customers. They also came to realize that privatization will help reduce government deficits and subsidies, improve their balance-of-payments and help pay their debts to international financial institutions. These debts have a negative impact on the privatization process in the Latin American countries.[34]

Privatization in Africa, has been slower than in Asia and Latin America for the following reasons:

1. political disagreements among different factions within the country concerning the privatization of national strategic industries, which are symbols of pride;
2. lack of capital and lack of financial infrastructure within those countries;
3. lack of knowledge as to how to privatize;
4. and lack of potential buyers among the nationals.

Limited or nonexistent capital markets in Sub-Saharan African countries is another big issue. There are only five countries that have shown signs of developing a capital market infrastructure: Kenya, Cameroon, Côte d'Ivoire, Zimbabwe and Togo.

René Springuel observes that three main reasons that have forced the privatization of public enterprises are: economic, financial and technical. Among the economic reasons, he cites the scarcity of financial resources after the fall of the prices of export raw materials and the high rise of external public debts budget disequilibrium and difficulties of public enterprises and low performance and lack of competition for goods and services produced by public enterprises.[35]

In order to privatize, developing nations need funds through loans from developed industrial nations and from international financial institutions. But because of the heavy debts that most of these countries have, in many cases loans have been refused. We come back to this point later. In some instances, the lenders may not be willing to privatize big projects in developing countries.[36]

The most feared constraint to privatization in the developing countries concerns the problem of who are the buyers of stocks in the newly privatized state-owned enterprises. Special-interest groups, such as ruling elites belonging to the same ethnic group and politically dominant one-party state, could be obstacles to privatization in developing countries.[37] In many nations, ethnic minorities such as "Indians in East Africa, make up disproportionate numbers of potential domestic buyers of public assets."[38]   In some developing countries, privatization has met some resistance when it meant transferring power and wealth from one ethnic or political group to another.[39]   This fear of concentrating assets in the hands of a few individuals from privileged groups is widespread and prevalent in Africa.   Callaghy and Wilson comment that these groups are composed especially of resident foreigners and politically disadvantaged but economically strong ethnic, regional or religious groups, which include "Indians, Lebanese, and Senegalese in much of West Africa; southern Christians in Nigeria, especially the Yoruba; Indians and Kikuyu in Kenya; Indians, Greeks, and resident whites, especially commercial farmers, in Zambia, and Indians, Pakistanis, Greeks, Luba in Zaire."[40]

We must, however, note that this practice is not only found in Africa but also in most developing countries.   For instance, in South Korea the government forbids any particular group to accumulate more than a small percentage of shares in any divested bank.   However, Leroy Jones, Pankaj Tandon and Ingo Vogelsang state that "the use of friends, dummies, and relatives has reputedly allowed each of the biggest business groups to obtain a controlling interest in a different bank." [41]

Because of the lack of capital markets in developing countries, multinational corporations and foreign nations have shown interest in participating in the privatization of strategic state industries.   This has increased and deepened the concern and fear of the nationals who view this as the beginning of a neo-neocolonial era.   The national pride of preserving strategic state-owned industries, the lack of potential national buyers, the problems derived from the special interest groups and the lack of capital markets have made privatization very difficult to implement, especially in the developing countries of Africa. Nonetheless, privatization is being carried out in these countries, especially in Cameroon with its bananas industry and in Togo with its steel mill, as well as in Nigeria, Ghana, Kenya and Côte d'Ivoire. We discuss two cases of privatization in Africa in detail.   The case of Cameroon shows a prospect for the success of privatization, whereas the case of Zaire shows how state-owned enterprises have failed.

PRIVATIZATION: EMPIRICAL CASES

These empirical cases of privatization focus mainly on Sub-Saharan African countries. Table 4.2 shows state-owned enterprises in Sub-Saharan Africa. As the table indicates, there were almost 3,000 state-owned enterprises in this group for Sub-Saharan Africa and the percentage of wholly state-owned enterprises is quite high.

The table clearly shows that the state-owned enterprise sector dominates the economies of these developing countries. This is also the case in the developing countries of Latin America and Asia. Wholly state-owned enterprises amount to

93.3 percent of the total in the Congo, 91 percent in Liberia and 77 percent in Mali, whereas wholly state-owned enterprises in Zaire and Zambia, with big strategic mining industries, consist of 39 percent and 57 percent of the total, respectively.

Table 4.2
State-Owned Enterprises in Sub-Saharan Africa

Country	Year	Total	Number Wholly State-Owned	Percentage Wholly State-Owned
Benin	1982	60	U	U
Botswana	1978	9	U	U
Burundi	1984	51	U	U
Cameroon	1980	50	U	U
Comoros	1982	10	U	U
Congo	1982	75*	70	93.3
Côte d'Ivoire	1978	147	23	15.6
Ethiopia	1984	180	U	U
Ghana	1984	130	100	76.9
Guinea	1980	181	U	U
Kenya	1982	176	47	26.7
Lesotho	1978	7	U	U
Liberia	1980	22*	20	90.9
Madagascar	1979	136	45	33.1
Malawi	1977	101	U	U
Mali	1984	52	40	76.9
Mauritania	1983	112	81	72.3
Niger	1984	54	U	U
Nigeria	1981	107	36	33.6
Rwanda	1981	38	16	42.1
Senegal	1983	188	U	U
Sierra Leone	1984	26	12	46.2
Somalia	1979	44	U	U
Sudan	1984	138*	U	U
Swaziland	1978	10	U	U
Tanzania	1981	400	U	U
Togo	1984	73	U	U
Uganda	1985	130	U	U

Table 4.2 (continued)

Zaire	1981	138	54	39.1
Zambia	1980	114	65	57.0
Total		2,959		

Sources: John R. Nellis, "Public Enterprises in Sub-Saharan Africa," World Bank Discussion Paper, no.1 (Washington, D.C.: November 1986), 5. Also quoted in Raymond Vernon, ed., *The Promise of Privatization: A Challenge for U.S. Policy* (New York: Council on Foreign Relations Books, 1988), 184.

Note: U= Unavailable
* Exclude financial enterprises

Table 4.3
State-Owned Enterprises: Share of Gross Domestic Product at Factor Cost

Country	Year	Percentage
Sudan	1975	40.0
Zambia	1979—1980	37.8
Guinea	1979	25.0*
Mauritania	1984	25.0
Senegal	1974	19.9*
Tanzania	1974—1977	12.3
Togo	1980	11.8
Côte d'Ivoire	1979	10.5
Niger	1984	10.0
Kenya	1970—1973	8.1
Sierra Leone	1979	7.6
Botswana	1978—1979	7.3*
Liberia	1977	6.8

Source: John R. Knells, "Public Enterprises in Sub-Saharan Africa," World Bank Discussion Paper, no.1 (Washington, D.C., November 1986), 7. Also quoted in Raymond Vernon, ed. *The Promise of Privatization: A Challenge for U.S. Policy* (New York: Council on Foreign Relations Books, 1988), 185.
*Gross domestic product at market prices.

Table 4.3 shows the state-owned enterprise share of gross domestic product (GDP). State-owned enterprise share of GDP range from as high as 40 percent in Sudan and 38 percent in Zambia to as low as 7.3 in Botswana and 6.8 percent in Liberia. Since it is a known fact that state-owned enterprises in Africa have performed poorly, this explains the large government deficits in those countries accompanied by misallocation of resources, mismanagement and lack of know-how to compete in the world market.

Table 4.4
Privatization in French-Speaking Countries

Country	Number of Public Enterprises	Date of Initiation of Privatization	Number of Enterprises to Privatize	Number of Enterprises Privatized
Burkina Faso	100	1987	12	-
Cameroon	171	1990	15	6
Côte d'Ivoire	140	1990	80	2
Djibouti	9	1991	4	2
Guinea Bissau	44	1987	9	2 ongoing
Mali				
Morocco	800	1989	112	7 ongoing
Senegal	xxx	1987	36	26

Sources: René Springuel, *Privatization en Afrique*, Rapport du PCRP IX (Washington, D.C.: International Training Institute, 1991), 2.2.

Table 4.4 shows a clear picture of privatization in French-speaking African countries between 1987 and 1991. Senegal leads the group with 26 state-owned enterprises privatized, followed by Morocco with 7 public enterprises privatized out of 800 state-owned enterprises and Mali with 7 enterprises privatized out of 60 public enterprises. Cameroon, which has a total of 171 state-owned enterprises, has only 6 privatized, but they have been privatized successfully, and Côte d'Ivoire with 140 state-owned enterprises, has 2 privatized. This table shows how slowly the privatization process is being carried out in Africa.

The most common form of privatization implemented by these countries were sales of assets or equity, joint-venture, management privatization and contracting out. These privatized enterprises lacked funds, and were unable to be self-supporting and their profitability, in all cases, were very weak or nonexistent. Some states, like Mali, have promised to use the funds derived from privatization to support their domestic programs in order to promote economic development and democracy[42] as well as to start paying external debts in order to attract foreign capital.

Based on the funds that are coming in through privatization and eventually through taxes from the newly privatized industries, states are making plans to repair roads and build new roads and bridges. They have started to subsidize small and medium entrepreneurs, to help rural farmers to grow more crops and market them to urban cities, and to build new schools and hospitals. People, for instance in Cameroon as we see later, are cooperating and participating in the privatization process because they have a stake in it.

Since in most of these countries the nationals do not have the buying power to purchase stocks, most of the acquisitors are foreign investors from the developed industrialized nations and the multinational corporations. However, the management of the newly privatized state-owned enterprises are allowing the employees to purchase shares.

Governments of developing countries are hoping that privatization of state-owned enterprises in the long run is going to reduce the chronic budgetary deficits and reduce external debts, and thus, free funds that will be devoted toward building economic, development and democratic infrastructures. This will also help develop capital markets. As we see later, this is why we support the view that privatization will bring economic development and democracy to the developing countries.

The lack of cash and credits and increased external debt in African and Latin American countries have resulted in the pressures from the World Bank, the International Monetary Fund and the major international donors to privatize the public sector. There has been very little interest shown by foreign investors for privatization in the developing countries, including the oil rich countries.

The developing countries of Africa, foreign investors and international institutions considered debt-equity swaps at some point. However, this did not prove to be attractive to international banks and governments.[43] Callaghy and Wilson state that Sub-Saharan Africa needs what privatization can potentially bring: greater economic efficiency, more extensive provision of services, "wider participation in the benefits of economic development and the renewal growth that can come from improved capital formation and investment."[44] In the 1970s and 1980s privatization programs have been pursued in these African countries with success and failure.[45] There have been painful adjustments[46] to privatization in Africa.

Table 4.5 shows privatization in Francophone African nations. The most popular form of privatization adopted was the sales of equity and assets. Guinea, Niger and Côte d'Ivoire led this category. Senegal led the group with twenty-five liquidations or closures, followed by sixteen in Guinea, fifteen in Côte d'Ivoire, eleven in Zaire and five in Cameroon. Another form of privatization opted for is leasing or management contracts. Togo led the group with eleven contract/leasing, followed by eight in Côte d'Ivoire, eight in Zaire, five in Niger and three in Cameroon.

Table 4.5
Francophone African Privatization by Type

Privatization Carried Out				
Country	Portfolio Size	Sale of Equity	Management Liquidation or Assets Leasing	Contract/ or Closure
Benin	59	2	0	-
Cameroon	67	2	3	5
Central African Rep.	20	1	0	-

Table 4.5 (continued)

Côte d'Ivoire	63	21	8	15
Gabon	40	3	0	-
Guinea	193	44	4	16
Mali	35	3	4	9
Mauritania	41	5	1	4
Morocco	84	8	3	-
Niger	33	22	5	3
Rwanda	37	1	0	-
Senegal	57	6	2	25
Togo	56	9	11	11
Tunisia	123	5	0	-
Zaire	45	1	8	3
Francophone Africa Total	894	133	49	91
Anglophone Africa* Total	829	23	23	20

Sources: Portfolio size: International Monetary Fund 1988; Alfred H. Saulniers, *Public Enterprises at The Crossroads. Essays in Honor of V.V. Ramanadham*, ed. John Heath (New York: Routledge: 1990), 133.

Africa economic conditions have been worsening; external debts have been skyrocketing. The developing countries of Sub-Saharan Africa need urgent help from the developed industrialized countries and from those countries where privatization programs have worked successfully to teach them how to go about privatizing. Sub-Saharan African countries need to put aside political and ethnic differences and really concentrate on the process of privatization, with the participation of the public and private sectors, and present their case to potential foreign investors. Arrangements could be made for the state to own the majority of shares and strengthen the management with educated nationals and expatriates. Whatever it takes, Sub-Saharan African countries have no other choice but to privatize the public sector, which has become too large. However, the national interest must be preserved in order to avoid political turmoil and ethnic conflicts. Everything must be done to make the public sector in Africa more productive and efficient and this can only be achieved through privatization.

The economies of Sub-Saharan Africa have depended on their mineral and oil industries, which are, for most countries, principal foreign exchange earners. These industries are state-owned. African economies suffered extensively with the oil crisis of 1973 and 1979 as well as with the sharp drop in the price of mineral resources, in particular copper, in 1973. This, accompanied by the recession in the developed industrialized countries of the 1970s, 1980s and now in the 1990s, has caused a decrease in the demand for African commodities. As the law of supply and demand dictates, the prices of these commodities decreased in the world market, resulting in high inflation, increased government deficits, high debts, negative growth rates, a decrease in the per capita income, and so forth. As a result, the gross domestic product (GDP) in African countries declined an average of 1.4 percent a year between 1980 and 1984, per capita gross national product an average of 4.4 percent annually and an import volume of 5.9 and export volume 77.4 percent.[47] In some countries where no study was done, the decline was even worse in the same period of time.

It has been said that in certain countries, such as Malaysia and France, that as the public sector grew, the rate of economic growth increased. This argument opposes our thesis in favor of the public sector. Paul Starr argues that it is not true that as public sectors grow, rates of economic growth fall.[48] And he argues that "in the process, whether or not intending to change, we are likely to narrow our involvement, interests, and vision of a good society and a good life."[49] E. A. Brett, on the other hand, comments that government should attempt to control its servants in state-owned enterprises and improve failed political and administrative institutions. Privatization should not be used as a scapegoat by the state to solve its economic and social problems.[50] The public sector has more civil servants than it can pay, nepotism is still widely practiced in most developing countries. Privatization can create more jobs, increase incomes and improve the standard of living. Chapter 7 documents our argument, and Chapter 6 documents how state-owned enterprises have failed.

It is widely assumed by most scholars that joint ventures between the government and the buyers is going to be the most desirable form of privatization in the developing countries. Based on these arrangements the government can be a majority or a minority owner. This joint venture aspect of privatization programs appears to be the best one, especially in the case where most of the buyers are foreign investors. This may prevent the government from nationalizing the newly privatized enterprises in the long run. The fear of nationalization still exists, however, depending on the regime in place. It often happens in the developing countries, especially in the case of a change of regime through a coup d'état, that the new regime dissolves the parliament and rule by decree. And in some instances, they nationalize the country's strategic industries as a means of strengthening their political power and gaining influence from the masses. In other words, politics will play a major role in the privatization process in the developing countries. Joint ventures between the government and private enterprises has been applied in countries such as Ghana where the state has a majority stake in 181 enterprises and a minority stake in 54.[51] In most developing countries, due to poor economies, joint ventures between the governments and foreign investors are hard to find unless the governments are willing to let the foreign investors supply most of the capital in the venture and provide foreign management skills, technologies, marketing and know-how.

The actual pace of privatization in the developing countries appears to be slow due to many of the factors discussed. For instance, during the 1980–84 period, of the 94 IMF-supported adjustment programs in the developing countries most of them contained policy recommendations relating to nonfinancial state enterprises.[52] Sixty-one percent of programs contained provisions for reducing subsidies to public enterprises and introducing prices that would cover operating costs while at the same time making a reasonable contribution to capital maintenance and new investment. Out of the ninety four IMF-supported adjustment programs, twenty-seven curtailed current transfers to state enterprises and eleven specified subceiling on credit to state enterprises. Over twenty-four of these programs expressed intentions for the divestiture of firms to the private sector; twenty-five of them included measures taken in order to improve efficiency and management skills.

WHO ARE THE BUYERS?

Since the capital market in the developing countries is not well developed and there is lack of financial systems, as we argued earlier, if there is going to be any privatization on a large scale, foreign investors have to be the ones to come up with the capital needed to finance these privatization transactions. Again, giving ownership to foreign investors may raise some serious political problems. This may be considered a return to colonialism where wealth was concentrated in the hands of foreigners. So, any government in the developing countries would try to prevent this from taking place if it is going to stay in power for a long period of time. As discussed earlier, many interest groups who benefit from the public sector may oppose privatization all together. As Kirkpatrick put it, where liberalization is threatened, political and ethnic groups who currently enjoy the protected economic rent created by the system of regulations and controls will actually be the ones to resist privatization.[53] This shows how complicated the privatization process can be. Even in the cases where privatization becomes successful, and joint ventures are successfully established between the government and foreign investors, national interest must be protected or else these newly privatized state-owned enterprises will be subject to forced nationalization in the long run. In our research, we find that there is cooperation and collaboration between the governments and foreign investors that have acquired the newly privatized state-owned enterprises due to the fact that the society as a whole is benefiting from privatization. The privatization process must be systematic, step-by-step, and should not be rushed. When selling shares of a state-owned enterprise all the groups must be included: proponents and opponents of privatization, the general public, the employees of the enterprise being privatized, labor unions, the management of the firm being privatized, people from different ethnic groups who can afford to buy shares and, especially, politicians and members of the parliament. Since most developing countries are experiencing fiscal imbalances and deficiencies in their economies, the privatization process would work if it is carried out systematically and carefully, solving all the differences among the government, the potential buyers at home and foreign investors.

If foreign investors are interested not only in making huge profits but also in making an economic contribution to benefit the nation as a whole, building technological infrastructure, promoting economic growth, creating employment and improving the standard of living, then most of the objections to privatization would be overcome.   Then privatization would prove to be a process that promotes economic development and democracy in the developing countries. Then privatization would improve the performance of the former public enterprises.   Bureaucratic controls that existed in the public sector would be reduced, the number of unproductive employees would be cut and efficiency and performance would be improved. With all these, every developing country would want to push for privatization.

ECONOMIC, SOCIAL AND POLITICAL IMPACT OF PRIVATIZATION

In the process of privatizing state-owned enterprises, the property rights theory suggest that by changing the structure of property rights, a change in ownership will be brought about, which results in improved efficiency, performance and quality of goods and services.[54]   This change of ownership will also improve productive efficiency by imposing the strict discipline of private capital markets on the firm.   The   privatization process, if carried out successfully, would alleviate the public sector budgetary burden on the government. As efficiency, performance and competition increase, the financial performance of the newly privatized enterprises will improve. The performance of public enterprises has been too poor due to mismanagement of these enterprises. This mismanagement is so intimately tied to the dynamics of neopatrimonial politics, which Sandbrook argues "can erode bureaucratic norms and practices and introduce massive waste and undiscipline into the public sector."[55]   Based on different theories and practices discussed, it seems logical that privatization will bring much improvement to the economies of the state and better the lives of its people. Obstacles such as political differences and opposition from different interest and ethnic groups must be overcome. If the state is to be the instrument of economic development and modernization, it has to opt for privatization.

We argued earlier in this chapter that the developing countries inherited public enterprises from the developed industrialized nations during the colonial period. It is just fair and logical that these same metropolitan firms and powers help dismantle the public sector. Hence their cooperation and collaboration is sought and is needed to achieve the goals of privatization through an influx of capital in the developing countries. Western countries have to help strengthen or even create the markets in some developing countries or former colonies, markets that are presently thin, imperfect or nonexistent. Once markets are in place and there are capital and potential buyers as well as basic economic infrastructure, privatization can proceed. This is true in the case of the poorer developing countries, especially those of Africa. In some developing countries of Asia, Latin America and three or four in Africa, these mechanisms already exist.

The developing countries can no longer rely on the public sector to promote economic growth, economic development and democracy. Instead they have to turn to the private sector and encourage competition, efficiency, performance and increased productivity of goods and services. This will accelerate the rate of growth of the economy of these developing nations. Therefore, the public sector must become the cornerstone of economic growth through privatization. The growth of public sector activities must be stopped and this has been the case in a few developing countries such as Chile, Brazil, Argentina, Venezuela, Hong Kong, Singapore, South Korea, and to some extent Côte d'Ivoire, Togo and Cameroon. If the public sector continues to grow in these developing countries, poverty will increase as well as the dependency of these countries on the developed industrialized countries and on the international financial institutions.

In those developing countries where the political risk is too great to privatize in other forms, governments should proceed with the privatization forms of leasing and contracting of state-owned enterprises. The governments still maintain control and can avoid major opposition to privatization. This is especially true in the developing countries of Africa where capital is scarce and markets are imperfect. Those developing countries that have relied on market forces as the engine of their economic policy have grown more quickly than those practicing controlled economies by the state. In other words, the market economy is the answer to economic development and democracy around the world. And privatization promotes market economies. The privatization process, however, must be conducted slowly and surely since even the most developed industrialized nations, such as Great Britain and the United States, are experimenting with privatization. Therefore, privatization should not be rushed in the developing countries. Those developed and developing countries that have applied privatization are discovering that it increases the economic growth of these nations and gives more choices and incentives to the population as consumers of goods and services.

When any country, developed or undeveloped, is looking into privatization, it should consider not only the economic, social and political aspects of privatization but also the legal aspects. Peter Thomas[56] discusses the general and universal legal issues involved in privatization. In the case of privatization, the majority of buyers of shares of the newly privatized enterprises in the developing countries are foreigners. Also, the legal, tax and political issues must be examined carefully, especially in those developing countries where governments and laws change so often. Individuals or corporations may have bought shares or signed contracts, and the next day find themselves dealing with a new government and a new regime that may or may not honor contracts signed with the previous government or administration. In many developing countries, the court system is very fragile. So all precautions must be taken by individuals or corporations involved in acquiring equity in the newly privatized state-owned enterprises in the developing countries. This point should not discourage foreign investors because it has been proven that in some developing countries the economic infrastructure is strong and laws are still respected by a new regime or administration. This has been the case in Cameroon, in Togo, in Chile and in some other developing countries.

Developing countries involved in privatization must create an appropriate investment climate. They must install a legal system that would resolve any property disputes and guarantee property and contract rights.[57] The government must respect the law of the land and nationalization of private enterprises must not be a threat from the government in resolving disputes with foreign investors.

When applied properly between the government and the investors, privatization could prove to be one of the most important engines of economic growth in the developing countries. Even though some theorists fear that privatization will decrease the quality of social services provided to the society by the public sector as the private sector seeks to maximize its profits, the argument still holds that privatization is the best means to economic growth.

The multinational corporations (MNCs) have invested heavily in the strategic industries and have been participating in privatization of state-owned enterprises in both developed and developing countries. What is the role of MNCs in the economic development of the developing countries? Chapter 5 deals with the multinational corporations and foreign direct investment and their involvement in the privatization process in the developing countries.

NOTES

1 . Colin Kirkpatrick, "Some Background Observations on Privatization," in *Privatization in Developing Countries*, ed. V. V. Ramanadham (London: Routledge, 1989), 96.

2. Ravi Ramamurti, "Why are Developing Countries Privatizing? *Journal of International Business Studies* 23 (1992): 228.

3. *Fund-Supported Programs, Fiscal Policy and Income Distribution* Occasional Paper 46 (Washington, D.C.: International Monetary Fund, 1986). Also see, M. S. Ayub and S. O. Hegstad, "Management of Public Industrial Enterprises," *World Bank Research Observers* 2 (1987): 79–101.

4. Ravi Ramamuri, "Why Are Developing Countries Privatizing?" 226.

5. See Hernando De Soto, *The Other Path: The Invisible Revolution in The Third World* (New York: Harper and Row, 1989).

6. Ramesh Adhikari and Colin Kirkpatrick, "Public Enterprise in Less Developed Countries: An Empirical Review," in *Public Enterprise At the Crossroads: Essays in Honour of V. V. Ramanadham*, ed. John Heath (New York: Routledge, 1990), 25.

7. Raymond Vernon, ed., *The Promise of Privatization: A Challenge for U.S. Policy* (New York: Council on Foreign Relations Books, 1988), 8.

8. Paul Cook and Colin Kirkpatrick, *Privatization in Less Developed Countries* (New York: St. Martin's Press, 1988), 8.

9. See J. Toye, "Dirigisme and Development Economics," *Cambridge Journal of Economics* 9 (1985): 1–14.

10. Adhikari and Kirpatrick, "Public Enterprise in Less Developed Countries," 25.

11. L. Gray Cowan, "A Global Overview of Privatization," in *Privatization & Development,* ed. Steve H. Hanke (San Francisco: International Center for Economic Growth Press, 1987), 7. See also, Rufus Waters, "Privatization: A Viable Policy Option?" in *Entrepreneurship and Privatizing of Government* ed. Calvin A. Kent (New York: Quorum Books, 1987), 35.

12. See, K. Farrell, "Public Services in Private Hands," in *Privatization and the Welfare State,* eds. J. LeGrand and R. Robinson (London: Allen & Unwin, 1984).

13. Yair Aharoni, "The United Kingdom: Transforming Attitudes," in Raymond Vernon, ed., *The Promise of Privatization: A Challenge for U.S. Policy,* ed. Raymond Vernon (New York: Council on Foreign Relations Books, 1988), 37.

14. Thomas M. Callaghy and Ernest J. Wilson III, "Africa: Policy, Reality or Ritual?" in *The Promise of Privatization: A Challenge for U.S. Policy,* ed. Raymond Vernon (New York: Council on Foreign Relations Books, 1988), 179.

15. T. Killick, "Development Planning in Africa: Experiences, Weakness and Prescriptions," *Development Policy Review* 1 (1983): 47–76.

16. W. C. Baum and S. M. Tolbert, *Investing in Development: Lessons of World Bank Experience* (Oxford: Oxford University Press for the World Bank, 1985).

17. Cook and Kirkpatrick, *Privatization in Less Developing Countries,* 8.

18. Ibid., 12.

19. Ibid., 14.

20. *World Bank: World Development Report* (Washington, D.C.: Oxford University Press for the World Bank, 1988), 180.

21. See P. Short, *Appraising the Role of Public Enterprises, An International Comparison* IMF Occasional Paper Series (Washington, D.C.: International Monetary Fund, 1983).

22. John Heath, ed., *Public Enterprise at the Crossroads: Essays in Honour of V.V. Ramanadham* (New York: Routledge, 1990), 30.

23. Ibid., 31.

24. Ibid.

25. Ibid.

26. See also Richard Hemming and Ali M. Mansoor, "Is Privatization the Answer?" *Finance & Development* 25 (September 1988): 31–33.

27. See also Matthew Montagu-Pollock, "Privatization: What Went Wrong?" *Asian Business* 26 (August 1990): 32–39.

28. M. Peter McPherson, "The Promise of Privatization," in *Privatization and Development,* ed. Steve H. Hanke (San Francisco: International Center for Economic Growth Press, 1987), 18.

29. Waters, "Privatization: A Viable Policy Option?" 35.

30. Clyde Mitchell-Weaver and Brenda Manning, "Public-Private Partnership in Third World Development: A Conceptual Overview," *Studies in Comparative International Development* 26 (Winter 1991–992): 60. See also, James E. Austin, *Managing in Developing Countries: Strategic Analysis and Operating Techniques* (New York: Free Press, 1990), 123.

31. Cowan, "A Global Overview of Privatization," 7.

32. Amnuay Viravan, "Privatization: Choices and Opportunities," *Journal of Southeast Asia Business* 7 (Fall 1991): 1–11.

33. Paul Craig Roberts, "What Will set Latin America free? Free Enterprise," *Business Week* (June 15, 1992): 28.

34 See, Ravi Ramamurti, "The Impact of Privatization on the Latin American Debt Problem," *Journal of Interamerican Studies and World Affairs*34 (Summer 1992): 93–125.

35. René Springuel, ed., *Privatization en Afrique*, Rapport du PCRP IX (Washington, D.C.: International Development Training Institute, 1991), 2.1, 2.2.

36. See, John D. Schulz, "Top Lending Official Doubts Future of Privatizing Big Third World Projects," *Traffic World* 229 (January 20, 1992): 16.

37. Paul Starr, "The Meaning of Privatization," in *Privatization and the Welfare State*, ed. Sheila B. Kamerman and Alfred J. Kahn (Princeton, N. J.: Princeton University Press, 1989), 38.

38. Ibid.

39. Ibid.

40. Callaghy and Wilson, "Africa, Policy, Reality or Ritual?" 189.

41. Leroy P. Jones, Pankaj Tandon, and Ingo Vogelsang,*Selling Public Enterprises: A Cost-Benefit Methodology*(Cambridge, Mass.: The MIT Press, 1990), 177.

42. Interview with Ousmane Sidibé, Director, Agency for the Promotion of Private Enterprises, Government of Mali, Washington, D.C., July 16, 1992.

43. See Richard M. Moore, "Alternative Sources of Capital," in *African Debt and Financing*, eds. Carol Lancaster and John Williamson (Washington, D.C.: Institute for International Economics, 1986), 148–160.

44. Callaghy and Wilson, "Africa: Policy, Reality or Ritual?" 179.

45. Ernest J. Wilson, III, "In Africa, A Rush to Privatize," *New York Times*, 30 July 1987, 27–28.

46. See also Patrick Tardy, "Painful Adjustments in Africa," *World Press Review* 39 (February 20, 1992): 43.

47. "Financing Adjustment with Growth in Sub-Saharan Africa 1986-90," in *World Bank Report* (Washington, D.C.: The World Bank, 1986).

48. Starr, "The Meaning of Privatization," 39.

49. Ibid.

50. E. A. Brett, "States, Markets and Private Power: Problems and Possibilities," in *Privatization in Less Developed Countries*, eds. Paul Cook and Colin Kirkpatrick (New York: St. Martin's Press, 1988), 58.

51. *Country Report on Ghana, Sierra Leone and Liberia* (London: The Economic Intelligence Unit, No. 4, 1987), 15.

52. *Fund-Supported Programs, Fiscal Policy and Income Distribution* Occasional Paper 46 (Washington, D.C.: International Monetary Fund, 1986).

53. Kirkpatrick, "Some Background Observation in Privatization," 100.

54. Cook and Kirkpatrick, 19.

55. Richard Sandbrook, "The State and Economic Stagnation in Tropical Africa," *World Bank Development* 14 (1986): 327.

56. Peter Thomas, "The Legal and Tax Considerations of Privatization," in *Privatization and Development,* ed. Steve H. Hanke (San Francisco: International Center for Economic Growth Press, 1987), 87–91.

57. Madsen Perie and Peter Young, "Development with Aid: Public and Private Responsibilities in Privatization" in *Privatization and Development,* ed. Steve H. Hanke (San Francisco: International Center for Economic Growth Press, 1987), 175.

5

Theoretical Framework of Multinational Corporations (MNCs) and Foreign Direct Investment in the Developing Countries

INTRODUCTION

As discussed earlier in this book, there are six or seven commonly used forms of privatization in the developed and developing countries, including contracting out, voucher, sales of assets by government to private sector, subsidies, load-shedding, private payment, liberalization or deregulation and management privatization. Sales of assets and contracting out forms of privatization are widely used. We also argued that in the developed industrialized countries, equity could be easily sold to the public due to the buying power of the people. The sale of equity is a very sensitive issue in the developing countries since there are no developed capital markets or, in many cases, these markets do not even exist. This raises the question that we also discussed earlier, Who are the buyers of the shares in the newly privatized enterprises in the developing countries?

Multinational corporations (MNCs) have heavily invested in the strategic industries in the developing countries, especially in capital-intensive industries such as mining and transportation. Since multinational corporations have enough capital to invest in attractive state-owned enterprises that are potential targets for privatization, they have been interested in purchasing equity in the newly privatized enterprises. As we see in a specific case study of privatization in Cameroon, multinational corporations have been involved in the newly privatized state-owned enterprises through various forms, by purchase of equity, contracting in, or management privatization. Hence, an understanding of some concepts of the multinational corporations, what they are and how they operate is necessary.

It is the goal of every developing country to attain the highest possible quality of life for its people. That was Professor Vemuni Ramanadham's aim to help each country elevate itself to its full potential. Professor Ramanadham "sees privatization or marketization as he prefers to say, as one way of achieving that goal."[1] The developing countries need to bring about fundamental transformation of their existing institutional structures and state-owned enterprises in order to promote economic growth and development.

Many developing countries in Africa in the last three decades discovered that "the African socialism that independent leaders readily assumed would re-emerge when colonial era was terminated has failed to materialize."[2] Samir Amin argues that "considered as a whole, social reality presents itself in these dimensions— economic, political and cultural."[3]

In order to help solve the social, economic and political dilemma, most developing countries opted for the nationalization of multinational corporations operating in their countries. These developing countries hoped that nationalizing the multinational corporations and putting the responsibilities in the hands of nationals would bring economic growth and development. Discussing nationalization and social justice, Eric Leistner argues that "the real issue, however is not nationalization per se but the objective which its advocates hope to achieve, that is, a socially acceptable distribution of wealth."[4] Leistner states that the driving force behind the nationalization of foreign companies was a wish by the new leaders of these developing countries to gain control over all aspects of national life in order to strengthen their own position. He argues that "the power to appoint indigenous people as directors, managers and so forth provided opportunities for political patronage as well as nepotism."[5]

MULTINATIONAL CORPORATIONS: THEORIES AND PRACTICE

Raymond Vernon and Deborah Spar state that national enterprises have gone international, "creating networks of affiliated firms located in different countries that are united together by a common parent, draw on a common pool of resources, and respond in some measure to a common strategy."[6] The multinational corporations have invested heavily in the strategic industries of the developing countries through direct foreign investment. Several studies have been done on the questions of whether and how multinational corporations help or hurt the prospects for sustained economic growth in the developing countries. Joseph Gricco states that these studies address three central questions: "What is the distribution of gain between foreign firms and developing host countries? What shapes the distributions of gains between those two sets of actors: And, what policies should developing countries pursue toward foreign enterprises ?"[7]

In this chapter, we are interested in discussing the theoretical framework of multinational corporations and foreign direct investment in the developing countries as they relate to privatization. The multinational corporations have recently been involved in the privatization of state-owned enterprises in the developing countries. There has been frustration on the part of nationals due to the overwhelming influence of MNCs on domestic economic and political outcomes in the developing countries. Hence, local governments chose to nationalize as an attempt to reinstate public sector control over vital national resources, which kills the potential for private enterprise development at both the national and international levels.

What Are the Multinational Corporations?

The definitions of the MNCs and the theoretical framework that we draw upon are discussed next. There is a variety of opinions among authors in approaching these issues. The intention here is to point out some views of the MNCs and their foreign direct investments in the developing countries.

When we speak of multinational corporations, we mean far more than that category of business organization whose distinguishing feature is that they all happen to operate in more than one country. Joan Adelman Spero states that by "multinational corporation" we mean "a firm with foreign subsidiaries which extends the production and marketing of the firm beyond the boundaries of any one country."[8] Multinational corporations do not include large corporations—such as Lockheed or Grumman—that market their products abroad; they are firms that have sent abroad a package of capital, technology, managerial talent and marketing skills to carry out production in foreign countries. In order for these firms to operate efficaciously abroad, their international organization has to be very effective, and this impinges upon their management skills. International organization "can be counterproductive when management is of the wrong kind or is executed poorly."[9] In many cases, a multinational's production is truly worldwide, with different stages of production carried out in different countries. Marketing also is often international. Goods produced in one or more countries are sold throughout the world. Raymond Vernon defines a multinational corporation "as one with investments in six or more foreign countries and found that such firms account for 80 percent of all foreign subsidiaries of major American corporations."[10]

In 1960, David E. Lilienthal introduced the term "multinational corporation" to refer to corporations that have their home in one country, but operate and live under the laws and customs of other countries as well.[11] Brahash Sethi and Richard Halton define multinational enterprises as a mutation of earlier types of international companies; in another sense, they say, they are the extension of modern U.S. giant corporations into the world market, but without the necessary political and economic institutions to guide and protect them.[12]

Carl Widstrand and Samir Amin argue that MNCs are not only a category of business organizations whose main feature is that they all happen to operate in more than one country, but also "a rapidly expanding sector of the world economy, characterized by a revolutionary new system of production and accumulation."[13]

MNCs are known to have huge financial resources. They have state-of-the-art technology, they are very well equipped with research and development (R&D) facilities and they are innovators of new technology. John Dunning argues that MNCs "generally record a higher productivity and/or profitability, they are prone to engage in more international transactions and they are likely to be more vertically or horizontally integrated."[14]

Jack N. Behrman provides an appropriate definition of the multinational's role in international capitalist production: "a multinational enterprise is one that attempts to integrate operations and centralize policy control while conducting business within a number of national economies."[15] Foreign direct investment facilitates this latter objective, since it entails a form of investment denoted by a marked degree of external control and ownership.

John M. Connor states that "it is difficult to distinguish the ordinary operations of the modern multinational corporation (MNC) from private foreign direct investment."[16] Dunning cites many eminent authorities who have considered the two topics as equivalent.[17] The different distinctive traits of multinational corporations are simply firm-level reflections of the industry of national-level characteristics of foreign direct investments.

How Do the MNCs Operate?

John M. Connor talks about three different features of traits of the multinational corporations: First, the modern MNC is a very large, complex organization. A second feature of MNCs is a strong tendency to produce differentiated, technologically intensive products in relatively concentrated industries. "A final basic trait of MNCs is their rates of performance, as measured both by profits and by growth."[18]

Horst explores the question of whether the profit-maximizing assumption is the most appropriate for the multinational corporation.[19] His answer is that although profit maximization is very important for the operations of the MNCs, other goals such as finding new markets for their products, bringing awareness of the products to different people, territories and countries, seeking raw materials for their industries and so forth, are equally important. Edith Penrose suggests that MNCs are attempting to maximize sales, profits and growth.[20]

John M. Connor argues that a second group of theoretical approaches to the MNC may be considered an extension of the neoclassical theory of the firm.[21] This theory assumes that the firm maximizes its "discounted sum of all future net cash flows and yields the desired stock of capital as a function of factor prices, interest rates, tax rates, and the depreciation rate."[22]

Another economic element that needs to be considered in the theoretical approaches to the MNCs is "denationalization." Denationalization is defined as the degree to which a nation's industry is controlled by MNCs. "Denationalization implies the transfer of decision-making for industries to foreign centers."[23]

Several studies have been done on the multinational corporations and copper, such as that by Theodore Moran in Chile, Raymond Mikesell in Peru and Papua New Guinea and Richard Sklar in Zambia. Moran's study of multinational corporations in Chile "attempts to evaluate the interaction between foreign copper companies and a political system under great pressure for change."[24] His main concern is the behavior of Chilean political parties and numerous interest groups, and their efforts "to push, pull and shove the foreign copper companies into contributing more and more to the nation's welfare."[25]   Moran describes how the system of relations between Chile as an exporter of raw materials and the developed industrial countries as exporters of manufactured goods, with the multinational corporation in the middle, seemed to work coherently and perhaps even intentionally, "to frustrate Chilean efforts to build its own industrial base, provide its own national welfare, and promote the broad process of development."[26]

This would have some implications once the MNCs and foreign buyers are allowed to spearhead the privatization process. The main argument of this book is that privatization promotes economic development and democracy in the developing countries. State-owned enterprises have failed. Hence, governments of developing countries must privatize their state-owned enterprises. MNCs have huge capital and are acquiring these enterprises. A collaboration is developing between the governments and the MNCs due to the benefits derived from privatization as we will see later on in this book.

In his conclusion, Moran argues that in Chile, the continuing decline of political support for the U.S. copper industries among domestic groups of the center and the right was one of the major reasons nationalization took place. [27]   He states that despite widely advanced hypotheses to the contrary, "as the foreign copper companies expanded operations in Chile over time, they did not gain power, or influence, or allies on the domestic scene. Rather, their alliances proved most fragile."[28]

Moran states that Chilean resentment and fear of dependency led inexorably to the nationalization of the foreign copper companies, but it also dictates national strategy vis-à-vis the semi-integrated global copper company. As a result, serious misjudgments about "pricing, revenue from copper, and market factors imposed major economic problems for Chile and contributed indirectly to the political instability of the Allende regime."[29]   Moran argues that the Chileans failed to realize that, in spite of having nationalized their copper production, they were still dependent on international markets.

A cumulative shift is observed by Moran in the balance of power between foreign companies and developing countries, as knowledge, domestic technical skills, confidence and overall economic development rise and enable a host country to understand and perform the functions that were formerly restricted to the foreign companies.

In his study of the copper mining industry in Zambia, Sklar sets out to investigate the political capabilities of the multinational mining companies in the face of Zambia's hostile ideological environment. Sklar tries to determine how Zambia's political environment is being influenced according to the long-run business interests of the multinational corporations. According to his analysis, Zambia also assessed the need to link up with international trade networks more realistically than Chile did. Thus, even with drastic reductions in the world price, Zambia was better able to maximize its revenues from copper than Chile was during the early 1970s. Sklar details numerous adaptations on the part of the multinational mining companies to demands generated by government and domestic groups such as African workers, trade union leaders, and party leaders.[30]

FOREIGN DIRECT INVESTMENT

Private direct investment is investment by foreigners for the purpose of directly controlling the enterprise in which the investment is made. This term is sometime called "direct international investment," "private foreign investment," "direct foreign investment," or simply "foreign investment."[31] Direct foreign investment applies to ownership, whereas portfolio investment does not mean ownership, which remains in the hands of the developing country. Foreign direct ownership is thus the antithesis of state or public ownership, and therefore is likely to play a role in every privatization effort to one degree or another.

During the 1980s, most developing countries were affected by the decline in gross investment rates due to many factors. These factors include, among others, "falling prices for primary commodity exports, a decline in private external financing, the presence of a large stock of foreign debt and the implementation of adjustment programs designed to restore balance-of-payment viability."[32]

It has been recognized that private investment, foreign or domestic, does play a critical role in generating economic growth. However, Joshua Greene and Delano Villanueva state that "there has been surprisingly little research on its determinants in developing countries."[33] Mario Blejer and Mohsin Khan conducted a study examining the impact of government economic policy on private investment.[34] This study was conducted in twenty-four developing countries. The findings include that the level of private investment activity was positively related to the change in expected real gross domestic product (GDP), negatively to excess productive capacity and positively to the availability of funds for private investment.

Since private investment does generate economic growth and since state-owned enterprises have failed to promote economic growth and development due to nepotism, inefficiency and corruption, then the present move toward privatization comes as a welcome change. Nationalization has failed; public sector control of the economies of developing countries has done nothing more than contribute to increased poverty and misery.

However, private foreign direct investment has long been a controversial issue in economic development. Many developing countries claim that advanced industrial countries have always taken from the less developed countries more than they put in. Paul Baran and Paul Sweezy state that foreign investment, seems far from a means of developing underdeveloped countries (developing countries) but rather "is a most efficient device for transferring wealth from poorer to richer countries, while at the same time enabling the richer to expand their control over the economy of the poorer."[35] Hence, Moran asks, Is the maximum flow of private direct investment necessarily good for nations of both North and South?[36]

The sentiment of exploitation is expressed by many developing countries that have experienced colonial rule. These nations aspire to greater political and economic independence. They feel that sovereignty will be jeopardized by direct foreign investment. Samir Amin argues that "the association of Africa with the European Economic Community (EEC) under the Lomé Accords must be understood in the framework of the perpetuation of the neocolonial relationship."[37]

Commenting on a tremendous imbalance in the distribution of international reserves, Ul Haq states that "the poor nations, with 70 percent of the world population, received less than 4 percent of the international reserves of $US 131 billion during 1970–74, simply because the rich nations controlled the creation and distribution of international reserves through the expansion of their own national reserve currencies (mainly dollars) and through their decisive control over the International Monetary Fund."[38]

These developing countries are concerned not only with economic independence, but also with the development of their national economies. There are other grounds for objecting to foreign owned investment besides the fear of foreign control over national economic activities. Somsak Tambunlertchai states that "the profit maximization motivation of foreign enterprises, their reluctance to act according to the interest of the host country, and their ability to avoid the control imposed by the host government are often alleged to have a damaging effect on the host economy."[39]

For the developing countries of Africa, the most disturbing aspects of the involvement of multinational corporations in their economies are the following:

1. the subsidiaries of foreign corporations have a strong impact on some extractive or industrial sectors as well as some services (banking and international transportation) in which no effective counterweight mechanism exists;

2. through their participation in the host economy and their transfer of productive resources, international corporations tend to become important channels for the transfer of consumption patterns and values that may affect a country's style of life;

3. the transfer of technology through international corporations is not always beneficial to a local economy and may in some cases even hamper the development of a country's own technology;

4. by operating in high-profit sectors, international corporations impede local entrepreneurs or, what is even worse, contribute to their displacement (through the purchase of enterprises).[40]

Another fear is that foreign direct investment affects the balance-of-payments of host country. When the profitability of operations of foreign investments is high, there may be a heavy transfer of profits from the host country to the MNCs, and when the opportunity to obtain profits is exhausted, there may be a withdrawal of capital funds for use elsewhere. Worse still, there may be a repatriation of capital originally invested together with the accumulated gains, which may exert an excessive burden on the balance-of-payments and jeopardize the economic stability of the host country. Another frequent criticism is that foreign investment increases the host country's dependence on other countries.[41] Based on all these facts, one would wonder if foreign direct investment from the industrialized countries of the North really contribute to sustained economic growth of the South. Moran states that "foreign investment can aid economic development if it contributes more to national income than it extracts."[42] He argues that only a very significant minority of foreign projects do not make a positive contribution, the majority of foreign projects do. However, Dennis Encarnation and Louis Wells conclude that"to date, the empirical evidence for determining the impact of foreign investment on economic development remains rather weak."[43]

It has been argued by many scholars that proof of the effects of multinational corporations' investments on host countries is still rather sketchy. This is so in spite of the many studies that have been undertaken. The most comprehensive to date is one directed by Grant Reuber for the Organization for Economic Cooperation and Development.[44] The Reuber study examines eighty foreign investment projects emanating from eight industrialized countries and placed in thirty developing host countries, among them African states. The study carefully incorporates the evidence from many other studies of the effects of foreign direct investment. Despite a number of favorable conclusions about foreign investment, the study does not provide a satisfactory answer to whether the overall effect of foreign investment in developing countries is positive or negative. Foreign investors do buy a significant amount of local goods, although the export-oriented projects buy less than the projects serving local markets. Others also have found a similar pattern, in comparison with local firms. Reuber suggests that multinational firms pay more than the going wage rate. This creates a privileged class in the host country. He argues that foreign investment does not significantly displace local capital, although the evidence is hardly conclusive. He suggests that his and other studies say little about the effect of foreign investment on local entrepreneurship.

In most cases, it has been argued that foreign direct investment is helpful to economic development. It is the desire of every developing country to improve its economic status. One solution is "industrialization." In fact, the term industrialization has often been viewed synonymously with "economic development."

Direct foreign investment, especially in extraction or manufacturing is, in turn, believed to be an effective means to achieve industrialization. In this positive or favorable view of foreign direct investment, two types of benefits are emphasized: the augmentation of capital formation and the transplantation of technological knowledge. One characteristic of the developing countries is the low level of income resulting in a low level of saving and investment necessary to generate a satisfactory rate of growth. Foreign investment is considered a preferred form of obtaining external funds. It not only provides additional capital but also carries with it a movement of managerial skills, technological knowledge and often some specific kind of resources into the host country. It has also been proven that additional production resulting from foreign investment can lead to an additional earning or saving of foreign exchange, for the investment is generally engaged in exporting or import-substituting activity. This positive or favorable view of foreign direct investment thus leads to a view that a country will be able to achieve a more rapid rate of economic growth if more foreign investment can be induced.

Developing countries striving to attract foreign investments are facing problems such as small market size, lack of infrastructural facilities and skilled labor, underdeveloped capital market and above all inherent economic and political instability. Governments of developing countries have taken certain measures to induce more foreign investment, such as protective tariffs or import duties on equipment and materials, guarantee of remittance of foreign exchange and exemption from income tax for a certain period of time.

Private foreign investors are interested in maximizing profits, although foreign direct investment seems to be able to supply some factors that are wanted for economic development. One major objective of the MNCs is to maximize profits. Talking about the objectives of the multinational corporation, Joseph Galbraith states that "The first requirement is a secure earnings record. Any firm that fails to do this is a dog."[45] Given a secure level of earnings, the esteemed firms are those that are large, that have a record of achieved growth or that are growing with particular speed. Increasingly, esteem is associated with the latter, and if a firm has a reputation for technological innovation, it is additionally known as a smart outfit.

Thereafter, a dividend record will be maintained. Michael Brooks and Lee Remmers, in their empirical study, confirmed that the managers view long-term profit maximization as the primary goal.[46]

The aim of the multinational corporation is to strive for a global optimization strategy to maximize profits of the organization as a whole instead of allowing each subsidiary to maximize its profits while ignoring profit interdependencies within the organization. Samuel A. Morley argued that global optimization involves complex management problems that are not associated with domestic operations: foreign exchange, risks, differential tax zones and costs of money, accounting for host country government demands, input sourcing as well as market allocation.[47] Morley and Steven Hymer argue that since stockholders are generally located in the home country, the corporate's first loyalty is to their interests. Dividends ultimately must accrue in the home market. This difference, state Morley and Steven Hymer, builds into global operations, a geographic flow of returns and forms the basis of conflicts of interest over returns with host countries.

Richard Caves and Hymer have stated that the causes of direct foreign investment are imperfections in international and national markets.[48] Foreign direct investment involves a movement of factors of production other than capital, such as skilled labor, technological knowledge and management. It also differs from domestic investment in that a business firm investing in a foreign country has to face environmental factors different from those in its own country.

As far as theories of foreign direct investment are concerned, Hymer[49] and Kindleberger emphasize the monopolistic elements of foreign investment. The essence of the theory is that, for a firm investing in foreign countries, there exist additional costs due to operating at a distance and costs of uncertainty and misunderstanding. The firm must be able to earn a higher rate of return than if it were investing at home. Another explanation of motivation to invest abroad treats foreign direct investment as a product of general drive for growth of the firm.

Bella Balassa, for instance, argues that the motives of foreign direct investment can be considered as part of the firm's market strategy in an attempt to improve or defend its position in both foreign and domestic markets.[50] Richard Caves, in turn, points out that the overwhelming portion of direct investment today involves either horizontal expansion to produce the same or similar lines of goods abroad, or vertical integration backward into the production of raw materials.[51] Somsak Tambunlertchai states that although the horizontal foreign investment may be motivated by the drive for expansion of the firm and may be influenced by protective tariffs in foreign markets, "the motive for the vertical foreign investment in raw materials is often for a better control of input sources."[52]

Bandera, White, Mikesell and Stevens point out that among the factors considered to influence the flow of foreign direct investment, the size of market of the investment receiving country and differences in returns between domestic and foreign investment seem to be the most popular explanatory variables. Other explanatory variables include exports to the country receiving the investment, tariff and wage differentials and different rates of inflation between the investing and host countries. [53] If successfully operated, international investment can lead to a more efficient utilization of world resources, an increase in world output and a promotion of the welfare of people in both investing and recipient countries.

Multinational corporations have opted for new forms of foreign investment. These are indeed forms of privatization discussed earlier in the book. Among the new forms of foreign investment are "joint ventures in which foreign equity does not exceed 50 percent, licensing agreements, management contracts, franchising, turnkey and product in hand contracts, production sharing and risk-service contract, and international subcontracting."[54] Under these forms of foreign investment, the multinational corporations of the industrialized developed countries have become heavily involved in the privatization process of the strategic industries of the developing countries.

We are not advocating the idea that selling state-owned enterprises to multinational corporations is an unqualified necessity, everywhere, in every sector. There are foreseeable negative consequences that must be avoided. For instances, MNC investments in mining, oil and transportation industries in the developing countries may cause some serious political turmoil and social unrest. Government officials may be accused of selling out to foreign investors for their own benefits.

The interest of the multinational corporations in the strategic state-owned enterprises of the developing countries has caused policymakers and the nationals in developing countries to raise some very sensitive economic, political and social concerns. The participation in the privatization of these enterprises by the multinational corporations must be carefully examined and evaluated by the governments of the developing countries. The interest of the population that has become so poor during the post-independence era, the sustained economic growth, on one hand, and the profit maximization by the multinational corporations, on the other hand, must be carefully weighed by the concerned parties in order for the privatization process to succeed. In the end, as Vernon and Spar argue, the most formidable obstacles to international cooperation on multinational enterprises may prove to "be political rather than economic: an unwillingness on the part of the governments to dilute their control over what they may regard as a potent instrument of the state."[55]

In our case studies of privatization in the developing countries, and in particular the case of Cameroon, we found that there has not been any conflict between the MNCs who have acquired the newly privatized state-owned enterprises and the host country.[56] Employees of the newly privatized enterprises participate in profit sharing, and are allowed to purchase stocks, as we see later. The MNCs that have purchased the state-owned enterprises are indeed contributing to economic development and growth in Cameroon. As we see in the case of Cameroon and other developing countries, the governments are using the proceeds derived from privatization, and are investing them in domestic programs in order to build economic and democratic infrastructures that are of benefit to these developing nations. Hence, developing countries should continue to privatize state-owned enterprises. In most cases, state-owned enterprises have failed.

Chapter 7 discusses the case of Zaire and how state-owned enterprises have failed.

NOTES

1. Christopher McIntosh, "Privatization Pundit," *World Development* 4 (January 1991): 28.
2. Robert E. Mazur, ed., *Breaking The Link: Development Theory and Practice in Southern Africa* (Trenton, N. J.: Africa World Press, 1990), 11.
3. Samir Amin, "Peace, National and Regional Security and Development: Some Reflections on the African Experience," in *Breaking The Link: Development Theory and Practice in Southern Africa*, ed. Robert Mazur (Trenton, N. J.: Africa World Press, 1990), 15.
4. Erich Leistner, "Nationalization and Social Justice," *Africa Insight* 20 (1990): 2.
5. Ibid.
6. Raymond Vernon and Deborah L. Spar, *Beyond Globalism: Remaking American Foreign Economic Policy* (New York: Free Press, 1989), 110.
7. Joseph M. Grico, "Foreign Investment and Development: Theories and Evidence," in *Investing in Development: New Roles for Private Capital?* ed. Theodore Moran (New Brunswick: Transaction Books, 1986), 21.
8. Joan A. Spero, *The Politics of International Economic Relations* (New York: St. Martin's Press, 1977), 89.
9. Giulio M. Gallarotti, " The Limits of International Organization: Systematic Failure in the Management of International Relations," *International Organization* 45 (Spring 1991): 183.
10. Raymond Vernon, *Sovereignty at Bay: The Multinational Spread of U.S. Enterprise* (New York: Basic Books, 1971) , 11.
11. For more information on this issue, see Richard L. Sklar, *Corporate Power in an African State* (Berkeley: University of California Press, 1975).

12. Brahash S. Sethi and Richard H. Halton, *Politics, Operations and Research,* "Management of the Multinationals," Symposium sponsored by the School of Business Administration of California, Berkeley, July 1972, 12.

13. Carl Widstrand and Samir Amin, *Multinational Firms in Africa* (Uppsala: Scandinavian Institute of African Studies and the African Institute for Economic Development and Planning, 1975), 29.

14. John H. Dunning, ed., *Multinational Enterprises, Economic Structure and International Competitiveness* (New York: John Wiley & Sons, 1985), 407.

15. Sklar, *Corporate Power in an African State, 2.*

16. John M. Connor, *The Market Power of Multinationals* (New York: Praeger Publishers, 1977), 2.

17. John Dunning, *Economic Analysis and the Multinational Enterprise* (London: The Gresham Press, 1974), 9-10.

18. Connor, *The Market Power of Multinationals,* 9-10

19. For more information on Horst's view on the multinational corporations, see Connor, *The Market Power of Multinationals,* 20.

20. For more information , see Edith T. Penrose, "The State and Multinational Enterprises in Less Developed Countries," in *The Multinational Enterprises,* ed. John Dunning (New York: Praeger Publishers, 1971).

21. Connor, *The Market Power of Multinationals,* 21.

22. Ibid.

23. Richard S. Newfarmer and Willard F. Mueller, *Multinational Corporations in Brazil and Mexico, Structural Sources of Economic and Noneconomic Power,* A Report to the Subcommittee on Multinational Corporations on the Committee on Foreign Relations, (U.S. Senate, Washington, D.C., Government Printing Office, 1975), 22.

24. Jeffrey Leonard, "Multinational Corporations and Politics in Developing Countries" *World Politics* 32, no. 3 (April 1980): 465.

25. Theodore Moran, "Transnational Strategies of Protection and Defense by Multinational Corporations Spreading the Risk and Raising the Cost for Nationalization in Natural Resources," *International Organization* 27 (Spring 1973): 55.

26. Theodore Moran, *Multinational Corporations and the Politics of Dependence: Copper in Chile* (Princeton, N. J.: Princeton University Press, 1977), 63.

27. For more details, see Moran, *Multinational Corporations and the Politics of Dependence: Copper in Chile,* 121.

28. Ibid., 10.

29. Jeffrey Leonard, "Multinational Corporations and Politics in Developing Countries," 469.

30. Sklar, *Corporate Power in an African State,* 96–133.

31. John H. Adler, ed., *Capital Movement and the Economic Development* (New York: St. Martin's Press, 1967), 187–88.

32. Joshua Greene and Delano Villanueva, "Private Investment in Developing Countries: An Empirical Analysis," Staff Papers, Vol. 38, No. 1 (Washington, D.C.: International Monetary Fund, (March 1991), 34.

33. Ibid., 34–35.

34. Mario I. Blejer, and Mohsin S. Khan, "Government Policy and Private Investment in Developing Countries," Staff Papers, Vol. 31 (Washington, D.C.: International Monetary Fund, (June 1984), 379–403.

35. Paul A. Baran and Paul M. Sweezy, "Notes on the Theory of Imperialism," in *Problems of Economic Dynamics and Planning: Essays in Honor of Michal Kalecki* (Warsaw: Polish Scientific Publishers, 1964), 20.

36. Theodore H. Moran, *Investing in Development: New Roles for Private Capital* (New Brunswick: Transaction Books, 1986), 4.

37. Amin, "Peace, National and Regional Security and Development: Some Reflections on the African Experience," 32.

38. Ul Mahbub Haq, "A View from the South: The Second Phase of the North-South Dialogue," in *The Struggle for Economic Development: Readings in Problems and Policies* ed. Michael P. Todaro (New York: Longman, 1983), 385.

39. Somsak Tambunlertchai, "Foreign Direct Investment in Thailand's Manufacturing Industry," Ph.D. dissertation, Department of Economics, Duke University, 1975, 3.

40. Felix Pena, "Multinational Enterprises and North-South Relations," in *Beyond Dependency, The Developing World Speak Out* eds. Guy F. Erb and Valariana Kallab (New York: Overseas Development Council, 1975), 68-89.

41. For more information on this issue, see Charles Goodsell, *The American Corporation and the Peruvian Politics* (Cambridge, Mass.: Harvard University Press, 1974).

42. Moran, *Investing in Development: New Roles for Private Capital?* 21.

43. Dennis J. Encarnation and Louis T. Wells, Jr., "Evaluating Foreign Investment," in *Investing in Development: New Roles for Private Capital?* ed. Theodore H. Moran (New Brunswick: Transaction Books, 1986), 61.

44. For more details on Reuber's study, see Grant L. Reuber, *Private Foreign Investment in Development* (Oxford: Clarendon Press, 1973).

45. Joseph K. Galbraith, *The New Industrial State* (Boston: Houghton Mifflin, 1967), 177-78.

46. For more information on this empirical study, see Michael Z. Brooke and Lee Remmers, "Organization and Finance," in *The Strategy of Multinational Enterprise* (London: Longman, 1970).

47. See Samuel P. Morley, "The Choice of Technology, Multinational Corporations in Brazil," *Economic Development and Cultural Change* 25, no. 2 (January 1977): 239-64.

48. Richard E. Caves, "Industrial Organization," in *Economic Analysis and the Multinational Enterprise*, ed. John Dunning (New York: Praeger, 1974), 21. See Steven Hymer, "Study of Direct Foreign Investment," The International Operations of National Firms, Ph.D. dissertation, Massachusetts Institute of Technology, 1960.

49. Hymer, "Study of Direct Foreign Investment."

50. For more information, see Bella Balassa, *Economic Progress, Private Values and Public Policy, Essays in Honor of William Felener* (New York: Balassa and Nelson, 1977).

51. For more details, see Caves, Industrial Organization.

52. Somsak Tambunlertchai, "Foreign Direct Investment in Thailand's Manufacturing Industry," Ph.D. dissertation, Department of Economics, Duke University, 1975, 14.

53. For more information on this issue, see Raymond F. Mikesell, *Foreign Investment in Copper Mining, Case Studies of Mines in Peru and Papua New Guinea* (Baltimore: John Hopkins University Press, 1975).

54. Charles P. Oman, "New Forms of Investment in Developing Countries" in *Investing in Development: New Roles for Private Capital?* ed. Theodore H. Moran (New Brunswick: Transaction Books, 1986), 131-132.

55. Vernon and Spar, *Beyond Globalism: Remaking American Foreign Economic Policy* 125.

56. Interview with Andre Blaise Kesseng, Economic Counselor, Embassy of Cameroon, Washington, D.C., December 7, 1992.

6

The Case of Zaire: How State-Owned Enterprises Failed

INTRODUCTION

The purpose of this chapter is to show how Gécamines and other state-owned enterprises have failed in Zaire. With its rich natural resources—copper, cobalt, gold, diamonds, uranium, manganese, and crude oil—Zaire should be one of the wealthiest nations in Africa. Instead, the case of Gécamines is truly a particularly striking example of the structural problems faced by state-owned mining companies in Africa and other developing countries of the world.

Over 85 percent of Zaire's foreign exchange earnings come from the state-owned enterprise, that is from the state-owned mining industry, Général des Carrières et des Mines du Zaire (Gécamines). Hence, the entire economy of Zaire depends on Gécamines. Gécamines is Zaire's largest employer and the number one source of government revenues. Revenues generated from Gécamines were to be redistributed in other sectors of the economy in order to promote economic development. However, the production of Gécamines has dramatically decreased ever since the Shaba I and Shaba II rebellions that took place in 1977 and 1978, respectively, when the ex-gendarmes Katangais temporarily took over the mining installations in the Shaba province. (In 1973 President Mobutu of Zaire changed the name of the province from Katanga to Shaba.) Since October 1991, the mining had stopped when most of the expatriate technicians and managers working in the mining installations left Zaire abruptly following a mutiny by Zairian soldiers.[1]

Production started again early in 1992 at the lowest production. In 1994 Gécamines, the state-owned enterprise, was barely producing due to lack of spare parts, mismanagement and embezzlement of public funds. Hence, the official economy of Zaire is no longer functioning and is in a state of disaster. Janet MacGaffey states that "export cannot keep up with imports, production lags, industry barely functions, scarcities are rife, the infrastructure has deteriorated drastically, wages are at starvation level and nothing works as it should."[2]

The international financial institutions, the World Bank and the International Monetary Fund (IMF), as well as all Western donors, have cut all financial ties with Zaire. The implementation of economic reforms set up in Zaire with the assistance of these international financial institutions have failed due to mismanagement and political problems that continue to worsen the economic situation in Zaire. Government officials control the economy and discourage other members of the society from entering the market. All the wealth of Zaire is concentrated within the ruling elites who also appoint the managers and officials of the state-owned enterprises.

The state-owned enterprises that constitute the backbone of Zaire's economy are no longer providing goods and services to the society. In 1986, Zaire had fifty-four state-owned enterprises that were mostly in the mining industry (copper, cobalt, gold, diamonds) and eighty-one mixed enterprises. As stated earlier, over 85 percent of Zaire's foreign exchange earnings come from these state-owned enterprises, mostly Gécamines. Over the years there has been mismanagement in these state-owned enterprises due mainly to the political appointees who had no know-how in the industries they were entrusted to run and due to the embezzlement of state funds. State debt assumption represented "a significant revenue drain of about $110 million a year in the mid 1980s or nearly 3 percent of GDP and 15 percent of total state revenue."[3]

In 1985 a central state buying company (SONATRAD) was created for Gécamines and four other state-owned enterprises. The IMF, the World Bank, and Western countries held a pessimistic attitude toward the creation of this firm.[4] A detailed study of the state-owned enterprises was conducted by the World Bank in 1986 to bring about changes. The Bank recommended the state of Zaire to restructure all its state-owned enterprises, privatize some of them, and put in place a new management team to operate the enterprises efficiently.[5] However, these changes failed to materialize due to the political opposition by some members of the ruling regime in Zaire.

Thirty state-owned farms were privatized between 1982 and 1986, and these farms were purchased by high-ranking government officials, their relatives and friends and their foreign agents. As we see later in this chapter, government officials, their relatives and friends acquired almost all the enterprises that were affected by the Zairianization measures announced by the President of Zaire on November 30, 1973. Detailed accounts of this are fully discussed in this chapter.

During this period of 1982 to 1986, big state-owned farms were bought by multinational corporations involved in agro-business. Zaire is also producer of crude oil, and in April 1985, PetroZaire, the state-owned petroleum industry, was partially privatized, partially because the state kept a minority ownership in four foreign oil companies that bought this state-owned enterprise. However, on May 29, 1992, the Zairian government announced that"it had seized the assets of all foreign oil companies operating in the nation."[6] The government of Zaire seized the assets of Mobil, Chevron, Royal Dutch/Shell Group and Petrofina of Italy. The cause of the seizure grew out of a dispute between the government and the companies over oil pricing. The seizure came at a time when Zaire was experiencing crippling economic problems.

Zaire's major source of foreign exchange, diamond, copper and cobalt industries, were operating at less than 50 percent capacity.[7] Copper output decreased from 470,000 tons in 1985 to 221,000 tons in 1991, and fell to even lower levels in 1992. According to Michael Heydary's estimations, Gécamines production was only 160,000 to 170,000 tons of copper in 1992.[8] Unit copper cost increased 145 percent from $0.67/lb in 1986 to $1.64/lb in 1991, with an average sales price of $1.04.

The World Bank, in cooperation with other international donors, has since the mid 1970s invested a total of $1.2 billion to Gécamines operations. These Gécamines operations contributed nothing to the economy of Zaire due to mismanagement, political interference and other events such as the Shaba I and Shaba II rebellions in 1977 and 1978. Gécamines has only one shareholder, the state of Zaire. Its Board of Directors are appointed on political merit and usually lack any managerial competence and technical skills in the industry. Gécamines has played the role of being the number one employer in Zaire with padded payrolls.

Several important economic and political events that have had a profound impact on the economic and political dynamics of Zaire followed the 1965 coup d'état by General Mobutu. After nationalization took place in December 1966, General Mobutu's regime quickly proceeded to take steps toward Africanization of the mining industry. We define Africanization as the replacement of the Europeans employed by multinational corporations (MNCs) with Africans (in this case Zairian nationals) in the key positions in the industry. Then, following his October 1973 address in the General Assembly of the United Nations in New York, in which President Mobutu condemned the exploitation of the poor developing countries by the rich industrialized nations of the West, he announced the Zairianization measures, on November 30, 1973. We define the Zairianization measures of 1973 as those measures designed to replace all expatriates involved in all commercial, agricultural, industrial (other than the Katanga copper industry, which was nationalized in 1966) and related sectors of Zaire's economy with trained and untrained nationals or members of ethnic groups. The Zairians were actually given ownership of all Zairianized business and industries by a presidential decree. These Zairianization measures, however, proved to be one or the major causes of the ethnic struggle and economic chaos in Zaire during the Second Republic.

AFRICANIZATION MEASURES

After the nationalization of the copper industry, the Mobutu regime was under pressure from the ruling elites to promote and appoint trained and untrained nationals and ethnic groups to the Board of Directors and key managerial and administrative positions. Zaire's new ruling elites wanted to control the mineral wealth of Shaba by placing nationals in these key positions of the industry, hence, the term "Africanization."

Was the Zairian government appointing nationals to key positions based on their skills or based on other factors, such as to what ethnic group they belonged, how militant they were toward the political party or to what class of the society they belonged? These are very important questions because, if these appointed nationals were going to control the mineral wealth of the country and distribute it to the members of the society, they had to be well qualified and technically skilled. Unfortunately, most of the appointments to the Board of Directors, whose members were the decision makers of the copper industry, were based on considerations concerning the appointees' political connections and ethnic ancestry rather than their managerial skills or their suitability for the job. This factor alone was crucially important in the decision making that severely effected the relationship between certain ethnic groups such as the Lunda and the ruling elites' ethnic groups. Tables 6.1 and 6.2 show the management of Gécamines, whose members became the decision makers for the whole mining industry. Note also that since nationalization in December 1966, the whole mining industry was placed under the sole jurisdiction of the president of the Republic, who had the power to appoint or fire any member of the management team.

In 1967 when Gécamines was created, it inherited most of the expatriates' personnel that were previously associated with Union Minière du Haut Katanga, the nationalized company. Table 6.3 shows a detailed picture of Gécamines personnel from 1967 to 1979.

In 1967 the total number of salaried staff was made up of 1,212 expatriates and 923 Africans. Among the 923 African salaried staff, 94.5 percent were Zairians and the rest were from Zambia, Rwanda and Angola. A year later, the percentage of the number of expatriate, non-African salaried staff increased slightly; however, in 1969 it started decreasing from 76 percent in 1968 to 73 percent in 1969. In 1973 it went down to 61 percent, and in 1974 and 1975 it decreased to 55 percent and 49 percent, respectively. It reached its lowest level of 498, or 26 percent, in 1978 and changed slightly to 600, or 34 percent, in 1979. All expatriate, non-African salaried staff were European, mostly Belgians, who were affiliated with Union Minière and Société Générale des Minerais.

Table 6.1
Management of Gécamines, 1978

Name	Ethnic Group or Nationality	Position
Umba Kyamitala	Muluba	President of the Board
Litho	Ngbande	Director
Liwa	Ngbande	Director
Charles Picquet	Belgian	Director
Norbert Rocher	Belgian	Director
Mozagba Ngbuka	Ngbande	Administrator
Bunhendwa Bwa Mushaba	Kivu	Administrator
Ekila Liyonda	Mongo	Administrator
Jean-Claude Nicault	Belgian	Administrator
Ttshambwe Dianda	Mongo	Administrator
Boboy Mokpala	—	Administrator
Statutory Auditors	—	Administrator
Mgandobami Egamo Keta	Ngbande	Administrator
Mutombo Mazeze	Muluba	Administrator
Atunaku Adunagow	Muluba	Administrator
KanindaPania WaTshimini	Muluba	Administrator

Sources: This table compiled by the researcher with the help of Ordonnance No. 78-231 du 5 Mai 1978, Parliament of Zaire, Kinshasa, Zaire; Ordonnance No. 78-339 du 6 Septembre 1978, Parliament of Zaire, Kinshasa, Zaire, and Rapport Annuel, GÉCAMINES 1978, Parliament of Zaire, Kinshasa, Zaire.

Note: The whole mining industry is under the jurisdiction and supervision of the president and the new ruling elites.

These expatriates still hold the managerial and technical positions in accordance with the agreements signed between Zaire's ruling elites and Union Minière. All the decisions, however, are made by the ruling elites and their appointees. However, all the expatriates were evacuated by Belgian and French paratroopers in September 1991 after looting and rioting by mutinous Zairian soldiers.[9] These expatriates have not returned. Despite the government's ambition to speed up Africanization of the copper industry, it was still clear that skilled expatriates were needed, and will still be needed for a long time to me. This is because prior to nationalization all technical and managerial positions were reserved for expatriate employees.

Table 6.2
Management of Gécamines, 1979–1980

Name	Ethnic Group or Nationality	Position
Umba Kyamitala	Muluba	President of the Board of Directors
Norbert Rocher	Belgian	Director - Administrator
Robert Crem	Belgian	Director - Administrator
Ekila Liyonda	Mongo	Administrator
Liwa	Mongo	Administrator
Buhendwa Bwa Mushaba	Kivu	Administrator
îNgongo Pembamoto	—	Administrator
Jean-Claude Nicault	Belgian	Administrator
Sambwe Dianda	Mongo	Administrator
Boboy Mokpala	—	Administrator
Satutory Auditors	—	Administrator
Atunaku Adunagow	Muluba	Administrator
Kaninda Pania WaTshimini	Muluba	Administrator
Mgandobami Eyamo Keta	—	Administrator
Mutombo Kambamwa Mazeze	Muluba	Administrator

Sources: This table compiled by the researcher with the help of Ordonnance No. 78-231 du 5 Mai 1978, Ordonnance No. 78-339 du 6 Septembre 1978, Rapport Annuel, Gécamines 1978.

Note: The whole mining industry is under the jurisdiction of the president of Zaire.

Normally, one has to have some professional training and a few years of practical experience in order to advance into the ranks of senior management. But in the case of Zaire, some individuals were appointed to key management positions through tribal and political favors. Many of them were untrained, and were appointed because they were members of certain tribal groups. This undoubtedly caused serious problems, resulting in the mismanagement of the copper industry and, to a certain extent increased, ethnic conflicts. Because there was a lack of well-trained African personnel, and because of pressure exerted by a competitive world market for mineral products, Gécamines began to support students at the universities and technical institutes in Zaire and abroad. Gécamines' overall policy of Africanization has been continued, and the progression since 1969 is set out in Table 6.4, which shows the university graduates in different professional fields who have joined the industry increasing, over the years, the number of trained Zairians in technical and management positions in the industry. These skills include civil engineers, medical doctors, lawyers, economists, business managers, accountants, technicians and other related professional fields.

Most of the managers of Gécamines listed in Tables 6.1 and 6.2 were somehow unqualified. The author has known these managers for several years. Some of them did not even have a high school diploma, very few had a college degree and most of them had no know-how in the industries they were entrusted to run. These were friends, relatives and foreign agents of the ruling elites. Over the years there has been mismanagement of the state-owned enterprises, embezzlement of state funds by political appointees and lack of goods and services from these enterprises to the population. These are good reasons why these state-owned enterprises should be privatized.

Table 6.3 shows a gradual increase in African personnel and a decrease in expatriate personnel, which would seem to be a good thing. Table 6.4 shows the number of African university graduates with various specializations, which gradually increased from 1969 to 1979. These particular years are singled out because that is the only period where the Zairian educational institutions were operating normally. Since the ealy 1980s, schools, colleges and universities have been operating sporadically. As of May 1994 all the schools were closed. Hence, the data presented here are the best we could gather for the purpose of this study.

The information contained in these tables has a bearing on the issues of privatization. If Gécamines were to be privatized, the talent, ability and know-how of these Zairian university graduates in different professional fields could be better utilized by the management of the newly privatized Gécamines. The way it stands now, most of these trained Zairians in technical and management positions are idle. The political appointees prevent them for doing the job they were trained for. These political appointees are used to embezzling state funds. In most developing countries, individual needs and wants are satisfied through corruption. In Zaire "corruption has been termed as structural fact, with as much as 60 percent of the annual budget misappropriated by governing elite."[10]

In 1973 the industry introduced personnel management centers. The role of these centers was to follow the overall training and promotion programs as well as each individual's progress. The industry had also organized some seminars for many Zairian employees. These seminars consisted of training in technical reasoning and analysis of technical problems, both human and administrative, and also stressed leadership techniques. Training courses in simple organization techniques were also introduced to the nationals for the benefit of foremen and managers with a view to increasing output.

Table 6.3
Personnel of Gécamines at Year End

Personnel	1967	1968	1969	1970	1971	1972
Expatriates—Non-African Salaried Staff (active)	1,212	1,581	1,458	1,415	1,409	1,384
Expatriates—Non-African Salaried Staff (on record)	1,212	1,733	1,657	1,637	1,622	1,612
African Salaried Staff*	379	547	610	622	720	820
Labor Force	21,752	22,262	22,348	23,530	24,586	26,648

Personnel	1973	1974	1975	1976	1977	1978	1979
Expatriates— Non African Salaried Staff (active)	1,297	1,238	1,136	1,109	998	498	600
Expatriates— Non African Salaried Staff (on record)	1,504	1,520	1,387	1,270	1,232	663	932
African Salaried Staff	923	1,240	1,420	1,652	1,790	1,924	1,893
Labor** force	26,520	31,597	32,840	32,567	3,2,149	31,660	33,000

Sources: This table compiled by the author with the help of Gécamines' *Annual Reports and Mineral Yearbook,* 1967–1979.* Among the African Salaried Staff, 94.5 percent are Zairians.** Among the labor force, 2.72 percent are Zambians; 1.44 percent are Ruandais; 1.24 percent are Angolais; the remaining are Zairians.

All this progress sounded great, but certain ethnic groups including the Lunda claimed that the ruling elites had instituted a quota system in the Zairian educational system. Certain regions, such as Shaba (Lunda), Bas-Zaire (Bakongo) and Bandundu (Bayaka), saw the number of the students from their regions entering the university and technical centers considerably reduced. On the other hand, the enrollment of the students from the ruling elites' tribal groups increased exponentially. This quota system is still being applied today, increasing ethnic conflict in the country.

Table 6.4
Africanization

University Graduates	1969	1970	1971	1972	1973	1974	1975	1976	1977	1978
Civil Engineers										
Africans	11	13	20	22	37	63	85	106	105	122
Expatriates	127	132	150	165	129	141	126	111	117	66
Doctors of Medicine										
Africans	7	7	7	7	7	21	21	27	28	32
Expatriates	26	31	33	33	29	29	30	34	36	33
Doctors of Law and other Fields (Business Management, Economics) and Accounting										
Africans	36	54	69	80	99	117	147	155	166	179
Expatriates	16	16	21	28	21	20	17	14	14	12
Technicians										
Africans	7	13	13	21	24	45	50	56	58	69
Expatriates	78	71	73	74	60	88	78	77	74	45
Others										
Africans	14	26	63	75	96	162	197	251	283	322
Expatriates	1	13	13	15	9	22	23	24	28	20
Subtotals:										
Africans	75	113	172	205	263	408	500	595	640	724
Expatriates	248	263	290	315	248	300	274	260	269	176
Totals	323	376	462	520	511	708	774	855	909	900

Source: Gécamines' *Annual Report,* 1978; Bureau Central de Statistiques
in Kinshasa, Ministère du Travail.

Another particularly difficult aspect of the Africanization issue in Zaire's
copper industry involved the treatment of the non-Zairian Africans who were not
recruited on expatriate terms. Unlike in Zambia, where the promotion of
non-Zambians to supervisory positions has been disallowed,[11] in Zaire, the
promotion of non-Zairians to supervisory positions has not been disallowed but
rather has been given low priority. During our field research in Lubumbashi,

Shaba, the Personnel Department of Gécamines, assured us that contrary to the situation in Zambia, as reported by Sklar, there has not been any discrimination in Shaba in promoting non-Zairians to supervisory positions. Neither the non-Zairian African salaried staff nor the non-Zairian labor force have been relegated to second-class status, as was the case in Zambia. Africanization in the copper industry of Zaire is being systematically implemented for all trained and qualified Africans. The only known discrimination within the copper industry, and a very serious case, which has increased tension among ethnic groups, has been the arbitrary appointments and promotion of members of influential ethnic groups to the Board of Directors and to top management levels through political favors. This has been a very sensitive issue that the ruling elites have failed to justify satisfactorily. These political appointees comprise a relatively privileged sector of the working class, and their annual earnings have caused a substantial increase in the overall wages, salaries and fringe benefits of Zairian nationals.

Two factors led to a rapid decrease of non-African salaried staff. First, over the years, the number of Zairian nationals graduating from colleges, universities and technical schools at home and abroad was becoming significant; chemists, physicists and accountants have been joining Gécamines' staff, gradually replacing expatriates. The second reason is that during Shaba I in 1977 and Shaba II in 1978, when the Katangais rebels invaded the copper mines of Kolwezi, 127 expatriates working for Gécamines were killed, and because of that incident, many expatriates left the country and were replaced by qualified and nonqualified Zairians. Third, after the nationalization of Union Minière du Haut Katanga, a technical cooperative agreement was signed between the government of Zaire on the one hand and Union Minière and Société Générale de Minerais (SGM) on the other. The agreement stipulated that these two Belgian companies would cooperate with Gécamines by providing it with technical and managerial know-how. The expatriate non-African personnel assigned to this technical assistance would be on SGM's payroll and their salaries were to be paid in hard currency (Belgian francs) and deposited in their accounts abroad.

This agreement between SGM and the national ruling elites was severely criticized by the opponents of Mobutu's regime and by the masses. They held that this agreement was a cover-up, enabling the ruling elites to transfer funds into their accounts abroad. University students in Shaba and the masses who knew what was going on protested against the government decision makers and requested some kind of explanations for this agreement. As a response to their request, the ruling elites closed the national university, all the students involved in the protest were drafted to serve one year in the army and the leaders of the opposition were forced into exile. Others were sent to jail for terms ranging from one to more than ten years.

The decision to close the national university and to recruit the students into the army, as well as the imprisonment of the leaders of the nonruling elites' ethnic groups, caused political disturbances throughout the country and many in the population, especially the students' parents, accused the ruling elites of ruining their children's future by denying them a college education while children of the ruling elites were in European and American schools. The petty bourgeoisie joined the masses in protesting against the 45 percent sales revenues agreement between SGM and the government and demanded the disclosure of the total amount that Gécamines had to pay as a result of this agreement.

The ruling regime became aware of the political and ethnic conflicts that this agreement was creating and made it clear that this agreement would end in 1975, but stated that it was necessary to abide by it since SGM had all the expertise needed to market Zaire's mining products abroad. The regime then made public the total amount involved in this agreement for the period of 1967 to 1975, as shown on Table 6.5. Despite the government defense in this matter, the opponents still maintained that these funds were being deposited in the ruling elites' personal account overseas.[12]

Table 6.5
Convention Payments*
(Z = zaires, $ = U.S. Dollars)

	1967	1968	1969	1970
Z	915,212.19	8,948,439.00	11,505,361.00	17,751,014.00
$	1,830,424.30	17,896,878.00	23,010,722.00	35,502,028.00

	1971	1972	1973	1974
Z	14,170,142.00	14,430,443.00	21,321,371.00	57,660,591.00
$	28,340,284.00	28,860,886.00	42,642,742.00	115,321,182.00

	1975
Z	63,316,263.00
$	136,632,526.00

Sources: This table compiled by the researcher with the help of: Gécamines', *Annual Reports*; Banque du Zaire *Annual Reports* Bureau de Statistiques, 1967–1975.
*Payments to Societe Generale des Hinerais under the Technical Cooperation Agreement dated February 15, 1967, as amended on September 24, 1969, and February 6, 1974.

During interviews with some high-ranking authorities of Gécamines and SOZACOM in Brussels, the issue of why Zaire could not gain access to the world market and sell its products through the London Metal Exchange was raised.[13]   Authorities said that SGM had a lot of experience in marketing copper and other minerals and had established contacts with some dependable customers over the years. Furthermore, authorities felt that it was easier for Zaire to market its products through the same marketing agent that had been doing it over the years.

SOZACOM was dissolved in 1984. Gécamines was restructured in the early 1990s, but its official corporate structure remained unchanged. Gécamines Exploitation is in charge of metal production, Gécamines Commercial, is the independent metal trading arm and Gécamines Développement in charge of nonmining activities.   These three companies, Gécamines Exploitation, Gécamines Commercial and Gécamines Développement are formally supervised by Gécamines Holding, whose Board of Directors reports to the Ministries of Mines and Energy, Finance, Portfolio, and the Governor of the Central Bank, as of December 1992.

The convention payments by Gécamines to SGM amounted to $1,830,424.30 in 1967 when the agreement was first signed. In 1969, when the convention was amended, the payment increased from $1,830,424.30 to $23,010,722.00. Then, in 1974, the convention was again amended, and as a consequence, the payment increased tremendously from $23 million in 1969 to $115 million.

What does all this mean in economic and political terms? It means that Zaire's ruling elites prematurely Africanized the copper industry without having the qualified managerially and technically skilled nationals to take over the top echelon of the industry. Africanization was costly to Zaire since it still had to depend on expatriates' skilled staff to operate the industry. It was costly to the ruling elites who lost mass support and trust. It further increased ethnic conflicts and also increased income inequalities between the labor force and the managers, who set their own salaries.

Table 6.5 shows payments to the Belgians firm SGM, which provided marketing for Gécamines. These payments jumped tenfold from 1967 to 1968, increased gradually until 1973 and then more than doubled. Zaire's ruling elites failed to justly explain the causes of this increase in payment. This substantiated the accusations made by the oppenents that these funds were being deposited in government officials' account in Europe. Members of this tributary class, as George Shepherd calls it, used their power to exploit their own people.[14]

Table 6.6 shows the wages, salaries and fringe benefits of both expatriates and Zairian nationals after Africanization. Overall, the earnings of mine workers had increased substantially during the Second Republic. They increased from $408,113 in 1967, when the industry was first nationalized, to $61,665,638 in 1978 for over 33,000 mine workers. During the Second Republic, the annual earnings of mine workers were more than double the wage earnings in other sectors of the economy. This factor has caused severe political tensions between the central government and the civil servants who earned, on an average, about one-third of the annual earnings of mine workers.

Sklar argues that comparatively low-cost African labor in colonial Zambia was the reason for the profitability of mining.[15] This also applies to the profitability of the copper industry in Zaire during the colonial period. But during the Second Republic, as shown in Table 6.6, the cost of mine workers in terms of wages, salaries and fringe benefits substantially increased. This increase in wages, salaries and fringe benefits of the African mine workers reflected a sustained improvement in their efficiency and productivity. The Africanization of the copper industry following nationalization had called for speedy training of workers, providing them with more equipment and, hence, causing an increase in wage earnings of the mine workers. This was not a result of labor unions. Ever since the state became the owner of the copper industry, all labor unions and all strikes by workers throughout the country were forbidden.

Table 6.6
Wages and Salaries of Expatriates
Wages and Salaries and Fringe Benefits of Zairian Nationals[*]
(Z = zaires, $ = U.S. Dollars)

	1967	1968	1969	1970
Z	204,056.81	389,439.36	524,989.92	714,720.00
$	408,113.62	778,878.72	1,049,979.80	1,429,440.00

	1971	1972	1973	1974
Z	941,760.00	932,160.00	13,069,053.00	24,013,556.00
$	1,883,520.00	1,864,320.00	26,138,106.00	48,027,112.00

	1975	1976	1977	1978
Z	27,147,173.00	44,125,047.00	50,245,964.00	62,079,399.00
$	54,294,346.00	51,308,194.00	60,537.306.00	61,665,638.00

	1979
Z	110,861,538.00
$	53,298,817.00

Sources: This table compiled by the researcher with the help of Gécamines' *Annual Reports*; Banque du Zaire *Annual Reports*, 1967–1979.
[*]These figures include: wages and salaries of personnel, personnel expenses and pension fund.

After Africanization of the copper industry, a new very difficult to deal with, problem developed—that of corruption and mismanagement of public funds. Quite often, ruling national elites have been accused of corruption and mismanagement of government revenues generated by the copper industry. Ruling elites and party officials have been accused of accepting payoffs from MNCs. Unlike the case in the developed countries, where the multinational firms try to maintain "a low profile if they can, and prefer to avoid direct contact with political parties and government authorities,"[16] in the developing countries, especially in Zaire, the MNCs in the copper industry work closely with the political party and the ruling national elites occupying managerial levels of the mining industry. These elites set up their own salaries with the revenues generated from the mines. For example, the salary of the top political appointees was "$15,750 per month, of political commissioners $12,250 per month, of government ministers $10,500 per month, and of generals in the army $3,850 per month."[17] The unskilled mine workers received between $35 and $15 per month. It was this issue of internal inequalities and the displacement that strongly infuriated the Lunda leadership. The fact is that ever since the Lunda Empire,[18] and even during the colonial period, the Lunda of Shaba and the Baluba of Kasai constituted the bulk of the labor force in the copper mines.[19]

The Lunda was a powerful empire founded in the early seventeenth century. The Southern Lunda, located in southern Zaire, established their firm leadership over the Empire by 1750. The Lunda Empire was itself a separate entity until 1891, when the Belgians, under the leadership of King Leopold, occupied the Katanga province without the consent of the Lunda Paramount Chief of the time. King Leopold became the sovereign of the Congo Free State in April 1885. On August 20, 1908, the Congo Free State officially became a Belgian colony (the Belgian Congo) until the day of independence, June 30, 1960.

Lunda heartland is rich in copper, cobalt, zinc, germanium, silver, cadmium, gold, tin and diamonds. The tribesmen of the Katanga region knew of these mineral deposits, particularly the copper, and they exploited them in a rudimentary manner. They made weapons and coins for the Lunda Empire. On June 30, 1960, the central government in Leopoldville assumed rights in the copper industry previously held by the Belgian government. Although most of the decision makers who set their own salaries were from the ruling elites' ethnic groups, the Lunda leaders had repeatedly seen this act as an exploitation of their own wealth, which they had previously controlled, by the new ruling elites.[20]

In 1971 the Africanization measures deepened the political crisis of the Mobutu regime at home due to mass rebellion. However, a year later in 1972, President Mobutu increased his prestige in international relations by recognizing the People's Republic of China. This recognition came just a few weeks after Former President Richard Nixon of the United States opened the doors that led to the establishment of diplomatic relations between the United States and the People's Republic of China. After visiting Peking, President Mobutu made a speech at the United Nations General Assembly in October 1973 condemning the industrialized Western nations for exploiting the developing nations through the purchase of their raw materials at very low prices. This speech was well taken by all the developing countries and this boosted, once again, Mobutu's political vision and political ambitions, which led him to announce on November 30, 1973, Zairianization measures by which all the foreign-owned agricultural, industrial and commercial businesses were taken away from their owners and were acquired by Zairian nationals. The central argument of this book is that privatization promotes economic development and democracy in the developing countries. Here again we see the frustration of nationals due to the overwhelming influence of MNCs on domestic economic and political outcomes of the developing countries.

ZAIRIANIZATION MEASURES

In this section, we present evidence that the Shaba region had more business and industries Zairianized than any other region in Zaire. We discover who acquired these major businesses and industries in Shaba and to what ethnic groups they belonged. These are the main issues we have to establish in order to argue that Zairianization measures were causes of the Shaba I and Shaba II rebellions, and that all these companies failed. Ever since, demonstrations for democracy have increased in force throughout the country.[21]

The information on Zairianization is based on original research in the field and, consultation of primary sources as well as secondary sources. During our field research we visited the provinces of Shaba, Equateur, Kinshasa and Bas-Zaire where most of the Zairianized businesses were located.

Ever since President Mobutu came to power, the regime had focused its attention on the total political and economic independence of Zaire. During the First Republic, a law was passed by the Parliament, the Bakajika law, named for legislator Bakajika who introduced the bill, stating that all land with all the resources underneath it belonged to the state. When the new regime came to power, it did away with most of the laws passed by the legislators of the First Republic, but it decided to keep and enforce the Bakajika law, among others. This law constituted the backbone of President Mobutu's November 30, 1973, speech before the national Legislative Council.[22] President Mobutu called for the total economic independence of Zaire. He made it perfectly clear that all large wholesale and retail businesses; all small and medium factories; all farms, plantations, ranches and quarries had been confiscated from European owners and multinational corporations and handed over to Zairian nationals or Zairian acquisitors.

These Zairianization measures created political crises later on. The main problem raised by the masses concerned who was to acquire what and under what conditions. In his speech, the resident failed to clarify how these measures were going to be implemented. He left an opening for a fight between his close collaborators, the legislators, the commissioners and the high-ranking bureaucratic elites. These groups were fighting as to who was to get what at the expense of the masses that were, here again as in the previous cases of Africanization, the main losers, along with the individual European owners and the MNCs. The concepts of class and ethnicity prevailed once more in determining the acquisitors. Here again the national bourgeoisie prevailed. Zaire followed the example set by other developing countries that had nationalized foreign-owned business activities as discussed by Sklar,[23] Collin[24] and William.[25]

The decision to Zairianize all foreign-owned businesses was not made by the president alone, but by all his close collaborators as well as the top ruling elites who helped him gain power. These Zairianization measures turned out to be the worst economic decisions that the government had made during the Second Republic, as we will see. The political and economic situation of Zaire worsened as a result of these measures. The European owners and the multinational corporations were given back their businesses in all economic sectors a few years later after the Zairianization measures failed. These Zairianization measures caused severe economic and political damage as regard to ethno-class conflict. We present a historical, economicand political analysis of Zairianization as it was revealed to us during our research through documents, interviews and first-hand information.

Upon the announcement of the Zairianization measures, the government instructed all the party leaders to start a campaign of awareness, explaining to all Zairian citizens in the urban and rural areas this important economic decision that the government had taken, that is, Zairianization. The people in the rural areas either got news too late or, in some circumstances, never got it due to communications problems. Some European owners and some MNCs heard rumors about the Zairianization measures before they were announced and had time to repatriate their funds and other important business activities, as well as the companies' confidential documents. In certain rural areas of Zaire that border the Congo-Brazzaville, Angola, the Central African Republic and Zambia, the Zairian acquisitors found the shops and businesses they had taken over empty, the European owners having taken all their properties across the border under the security of some national gendarmes whom they had corrupted. This further irritated the masses, who found themselves unable to purchase basic food necessities that used to be readily available in the rural business districts. Responding to the smuggling of funds and goods by the MNCs and European private owners, the government quickly proceeded to close all bank accounts of all foreign businesses and allowed only a minimum amount to be withdrawn in the presence of a government official for salaries, purchases of merchandise and day-to-day operation of business activities.

Who were the Zairian acquisitors? How were they selected? After the announcement of the measures, President Mobutu asked his political affairs commissioner, Citoyen Kithima, to implement them and select the future acquisitors with the last word of approval reserved to the president. The government had a list of all the major businesses, industries and shops that existed in every region or province, but ignored the state in which they were left by their owners. So the political affairs commissioner sent a long memorandum to all the regional commissioners on December 5, 1973, instructing them that they were to manage all the business activities in collaboration with their European owners, who were ordered to remain in their business locations until the new Zairian acquisitors arrived in the area. This memorandum never arrived in many regions due to communication difficulties in the interior of the country. All borders were closed to all European owners and managers of the MNCs whose businesses were Zairianized. They were instructed to stay in the country until the new acquisitors had taken over the operation of the businesses, industries, plantations, farms, quarries and shops. Meanwhile, in Kinshasa, a political debate was going on between the president of Zaire and his close collaborators, the legislators and the party leaders as to who should acquire what. Mobutu's collaborators wanted to acquire all major businesses and portions of land.

Zairianization measures did not promote economic development and democracy but privatization, if well implemented, would.

THE ACQUISITORS AND CRITERIA FOR ACQUISITION: THE ETHNO-CLASS CONFLICT

On December 3, 1973, the National Executive Council met to set guidelines concerning the distribution of all businesses and properties Zairianized. It was made clear after the meeting that the criteria for acquisition were to be party militantism and competence. But the Office of the Presidency had the last word in the distribution. Edward Kannyo states that "the rule of thumb followed was the higher one's actual or ascribed position in the country's political administrative bureaucracy, the larger one's acquisitions."[26] On December 5, 1973, Political Affairs Commissioner, Citoyen Kithima, sent a memorandum to all regional commissioners requesting them to submit the names of party militants in their region who they felt were qualified acquisitors. He made it clear, again, that no Zairian would acquire anything without the approval and written consent of the Office of the President. In order to help resolve the political battle that developed among the national bourgeoisie, the three most political institutions met in Kinshasa on December 26, 1973. The "Trio" was composed of the National Executive Council, the Political Bureau of the Mouvement Populaire de la Revolution, and the Legislative Council. This meeting was chaired by President Mobutu himself. Notice that all of the most important ruling elites, high bureaucratic officers and party leaders, were present, most of whom lived in Kinshasa, the capital city of Zaire. The interests of the masses who lived in the countryside and provinces, and who constituted over 80 percent of the population of Zaire, were not represented at all. This is one of the very important ingredients that contributed to political and ethnic conflicts in Zaire, and the increasing tension between the ruling elites and the masses. There was no participation of the masses; which is a key ingredient of democracy. At the "Trio" meeting, it was unanimously decided that all the major industries, plantations, farms and business activities that were considered strategic to the economy and welfare of the country would be taken over by the state. The remaining small plantations, farms and businesses would be handed over to the ruling elites, party leaders, the regional commissioners and to some members of the three political institutions. Here again we see that the government chose to nationalize strategic industries as an attempt to reinstate public sector control over vital national resources, killing the potential for private enterprise development at both national and international level.

ACQUISITION AND POLITICAL DISINTEGRATION

The two criteria for the acquisitions set up previously were militancy and competence. Most of these people selected by the three institutions were militant enough, but few were competent enough to run a business. The majority had never operated a business in their lives but suddenly became rich overnight. Here the situation got out of hand. The Office of the President decided that those who acquired businesses had to live in the area where the businesses were located. Yet most of the acquisitors were political party leaders who were at the party's permanent headquarters in Kinshasa, legislators who were supposed to be in session in Parliament in Kinshasa or high-ranking bureaucratic elites positioned in the civil services administrative headquarters in Kinshasa. It was particularly impossible for the acquisitors to run business and government or party affairs at the same time. Also, none of these national bourgeoisie, who were used to driving Mercedes Benzes, would leave Kinshasa and reside in the countryside. The acquisitors appointed their closest relatives, friends and members of their own ethnic groups who, in most cases, knew nothing about running a business, factory or a plantation. These untrained managers, along with the acquisitors, turned the economy upside down. The excluded ethnic groups were distraught. The untrained acquisitors got hold of all the equity and there was no cash left to purchase equipment, new merchandise and to pay salaries. Finally, within days, most businesses started closing doors and laying off employees. Even the population in the small villages were surprised by the rapid deterioration that happened within just days. The ruling elites became super-rich at the expense of foreign owners and the masses who were promised a better life and better prices for all the basic necessities since their own Zairian compatriots had taken over the destiny of the country.

The population became aware that they were being used and began political demonstrations and looting. The situation has not changed as of September

1992, soldiers as well as ordinary people have participated in these demonstrations and looting.[27]

In order to inform the masses, the political affairs commissioner gave a press release on December 30, 1973, in which he announced that all the acquisitors would be required to present income statements at the request of the government, and that the acquisitors were working for the people as a whole.[28] The masses knew that the political affairs commissioner was not telling the truth, and that he was only defending the interests of the national bourgeoisie. This infuriated the opposition political parties scattered abroad—among them the Front for the National Liberation of the Congo, which was on the verge of launching an attack against the ruling elites.

Most of the Zairianized businesses were located in four regions of Zaire: Shaba, the Equator, Kinshasa and Bas-Zaire. Among the regions of Zaire, the Shaba region had more Zairianized businesses and industries Zairianized than any other region in Zaire.

In Shaba, the Tshombe family had more businesses and plantations than any other family prior to the Zairianization measures. Under the Belgians, Joseph Kapenda Tshombe was "the most prominent African businessman in the whole of Lunda. He was the most successful merchant, plantation owner and founder of the family fortune."[29] His son, Moise Tshombe, inherited the family businesses and became the leader and spokesman of the Lunda tribe. The Lunda became infuriated because none of the immediate Tshombe family, or any other Lunda, acquired any businesses, plantations or industries after the Zairianization measures were implemented. Although they had owned most of the Zairianized businesses and had joint-venture agreements with expatriate businessmen, this family was denied this privilege. That was because the ruling elites still held the Tshombe family and his Lunda leadership responsible for the secession and other internal political disturbances that followed.

The politics of ethnicity continued to play a major role in the Lunda heartland. After the death of Paramount Ditende, Moise Tshombe, who had married Ditende's daughter, became the prominent leader of the Lunda. After June 30, 1960, the Lunda saw the privileges they had enjoyed during the colonial adminstration vanish. This happened because Lumumba's government in Leopoldville refused to include chiefs. Hence the Lunda chiefs lost their political and economic priveleges. On July 11, 1960, Moise Tshombe, concerned with the Lunda's lost priveleges and status, declared the total independence of the Katanga province. The independent state of Katanga restored the authority that the chiefs once had during the Lunda empire.

The UN troops were sent to the Congo on January 14, 1963, to try to liberate the Katangese from the mercenaries and the Tshombe government. Faced with military pressure from both the United Nations' troops and the National Congolese Army, Tshombe left his Katanga province of mineral wealth to seek exile in Spain in June 1963. This officially ended the Katangese secession. Since the Katangese secession, there has been tension between the Lunda and the ruling groups, composed of Ngbande and Mongo. Table 6.7 which lists the major Zairianized businesses, industries and plantations located in the four regions, shows that Shaba was the location of more Zairianized businesses, industries and plantations than any of the other three regions. This table also shows that private enterprise was quite unequally distributed, and hence at political risk from the have-nots. It also shows that Zairianization was very unequal, and hence demonstrated ethnic favoritism.

The distribution of the Zairianized businesses symbolized the ethno-class struggle. In a sense, the Zairianization beneficiaries, or acquisitors, followed the force lines of the Zairian class structure as well as the ethnic background. This class structure consisted of

1. the bureaucratic bourgeoisie;
2. the petty bourgeoisie; and
3. the peasants and migrant workers, which constituted three-fourths of the population.

Only the first two classes benefitted from the Zairianization measures; the last class did not acquire a single business. They were neglected for several reasons:

1. according to the government guidelines, they were not militant enough nor competent enough to carry on business transactions;
2. they did not occupy positions in any of the three national political institutions;
3. they did not have close friends in positions of power, nor did they belong to the ruling elites' ethnic groups;
4. they lived in the countryside and, for the most part, were the forgotten peoplesince all business and political activities were centered in the big urban centers;
5. the Lunda were neglected because the ruling elites did not care about them and they (the ruling elites) underestimated their political influence until the rebellions broke out;
6. the Lunda were left out because the ruling elites were too greedy and wanted everything for themselves.

We have discovered who acquired the major businesses and industries in Shaba and the other three major regions and to what ethnic groups they belonged. Table 6.8 shows the acqusitors and their ethnic origins.

The opposition to the ruling elites' decision to base acquisition of businesses on ethno-class grew considerably throughout the country. The members of the three national political institutions were accused of helping themselves instead of helping the population.[30] In his New Year's speech of January 1, 1974, President Mobutu assured the population and his political opponents that it was not his intention to form a new class in Zaire that benefitted from the

Zairianization measures.[31] The acquisitors were supposed to help their own people and not to exploit them. He announced in January 1974 that "all economic activities affected by the measures of November would be taken over by the state."[32] Hence, they all become state-owned enterprises, and they all failed. They were completely bankrupt. This shows how state-owned enterprises failed in Zaire,[33] which is the point made throughout this chapter.

Table 6.7
Zairianization in the Regions of Shaba, Equateur, Kinshasa and Bas-Zaire

SHABA	
Old Business	**Type**
Soco	Wholesale
Hasson	Wholesale
Mercado	Wholesale
Boutique France	Retail Luxury (lost)
V.A.P.	Bakery
Vovema	Hardware
Mobiza	Furniture
Marberie du Shaba	Quarry
Keshev Vital	Food
Bernstein	Jewelry
Angevan	Wholesale
Franco	Wholesale
18 Businesses	Wholesale and Retail
Tarico	Wholesale
Menasche Velo	Bicycle
Alimenza	Wholesale
Maessart	Retail
Vendome	Boutique
DeReusch	Jewelry
Danon	Wholesale
Schlitz	Spare Parts
Sparville	Men's Wear

EQUATEUR	
Old Business	**Type**
SCZ Binga	Coffee, Cocoa
	Rubber, Palm
SCZ Basondjo	Coffee, Cocoa
	Rubber, Palm
Bangala-Lisala	Coffee, Cocoa
	Rubber, Palm
Bangala-Gemena	Coffee, Cocoa
	Rubber, Palm

KINSASHA	
Old Business	**Type**
Bank de Kinshasa	Bank
U.Z.A.M.	Retail
Bralima	Brokery
B.A.T. Zaire	Shoe
SAPA	Retail
AZADA	Retail
UNIBRA	Brewery
S.C.A.	Foodstuff

(Table 6.7, continued)

Sideris	Hardware
N. Stanzos	Retail
P. Stanzos	Bakery
Mme. Toilette	Women's Wear
Radio Service	Radio
Maison du Disque	Records
Atadji, Paraytos	Wholesale
Levico	Wholesale
Bata	Retail
Deftersos	Wholesale
Piesauto	Bodyshop
Jeannaza	Supermarket
Blackwood/Hodge	Wholesale

BAS-ZAIRE	
Old Business	**Type**
Cimetarie de Lukala	Cement
Compagnie Sucriere de Kuilu-Ngongo J.V.L.	Palm

Sources: This Table compiled with the help of The Ministry of Agriculture and Planning in Kinshasa, Region de l'Equateur, Division Regionale de l'Agriculture, *Rapport Annuel 1974*, 88–89 and 132–138, and David J. Gould,"Disorganization Theory and Underdevelopment Administration: Local Organization in the Framework of Zairian National Development," Paper presented at the African and American Studies's Annual Meeting, Houston, Tex., November 1977, 60–61.

Table 6.8
Zaire's Acquisitors and Their Ethnic Background

Old Business	Acquisitors	Ethnic Group
Soco	Regional Commissioner	All these major businesses were acquired by the ruling elite ethnic groups, Ngbande and Mongo of Ngbande and Mongo
Hasson		
Mercado		
Boutique France	(lost)	
V.A.P	Director, Executive Office of the Preisent	
Vovema	Bureau Politique Member and State Commissionner	
Mobiza		
Marberie du Shaba	State Commissionner for Orientation	
Kashav Vital	Assistant Regional Commissionner	

(Table 6.8, continued)

Bernstein	Subregional Commissionner	
Angevan	Former Ambassador	
Franco	State Commissionner for Justice	
18 Businesses	18 Congressmen	
Tarica	Regional Military Commander	
Menasche Velo	Assistant Military Commander	
Alimenza	Retired General	
Maessart	Retired General	
Vendome	Leading company Director	
DeReusch		
Danon	Leading company Director	
Schlitz		
Sparville	Air Zaire Pilot	
Sideris	Tribal Chief	
N. Stanzos	Brother of Tribal Chief Assistant Tribal Chief	
P. Stanzos	Vice Chancellor, University	
Mme Toillette		
Radio Service	Editor, newspaper	
Maison du Disque		
Atadji, Paraytos	Editor, newspaper	
Levico	Established businessman	
Bata	Bank Director	
Deftersos	Director, CND	
Piesauto	Ex-minister	
Jeannaza	Ex-minister	
Blackwood/Hodge	Ex-minister President, Journalist Association Ex-mayor, subregion: head, JMPR	
SZC Binga	President and Ngbande	Engulu
SCZ Basondjo	President and Ngbande	Engulu
Bangala-Lisala (plantation)	President and Engulu	Ngbande
Bangala-Gemena (plantation)	President and Engulu	Ngbande

Kinshasa

Old Business	Acquisitors	Ethnic Group
Bank de Kinshasa	Dokolo	Musingombe
U.Z.A.M	Kisombe	Musingombe
Bralima	Dokolo	Musingombe
B.A.T. Zaire	Ngualaf	Mukomgo
SAPA	Bomboko	Mongo
AZADA	Wazabanga	Ngbande
UNIBRA	Dokolo	Mukongo
S.C.A.	Litho	Ngbande

(Table 6.8, continued)

Bas-Zaire

Old Business	Acquisitors	Ethnic Group
Cimenterie de Lukala		The real acquisitors of these businesses were the Ngbande-Mongo ruling elites
Compagnie Sucriere de Kuilu-Ngongo J.V.L.		

Sources: This table compiled with the help of the Ministry of Agriculture and Planning in Kinshasa, region de l'Equateur, Division Regionale de l'Agriculture, *Rapport Annuel* 1974, 88–89 and 132–138. Also, David J. Gould, "Disorganization Theory and Underdevelopment Administration: Local Organization in the Framework of Zairian National Development," Paper presented at the African and American Studies Association's Annual Meeting, Houston, Tex., November 1977, 60–61.

Zaire's political and economic situations reached their lowest level during the Second Republic, following the Zairianization measures. The tension between the ruling elites and the peasants and migratory workers increased. The peasants found themselves unable to purchase basic food necessities. On the other hand, the national bourgeoisie, that is, the acquisitors, were unable to manage their acquisitions, unable to supply them with new merchandise and unable to import parts and equipment necessary to keep the industry operating. The acquisitors quickly emptied the bank accounts of their acquisitions and had no money to purchase new merchandise or to pay their employees.

The Zairian population was divided into several camps:

1. Those who enjoyed the advantages and privileges brought to them by the acquisitors who were either their relalatives or from the same ethnic group;

2. those who had no relatives among the acquisitors;

3. the hated ethnic groups such as the Lunda.

Four years later, in 1977 and 1978, this last group decided to challenge the ruling elites by attempting to capture the mining region of Shaba. The second group, which had no relatives or people from the same ethnic group among the acquisitors, started organizing themselves and sent a message of disapproval of the Zairianization measures to the Office of the President, requesting that a portion of Zairianized businesses be allocated to the masses in the countryside whose small farms fed all of the urban centers in Kinshasa.

The severe reaction of the masses and of the exiled leaders came as a surprise to the ruling elites. On March 24, 1974, President Mobutu chaired a meeting of the National Executive Council. The purpose of the meeting was to bring a solution to the reaction of the masses. At the end of the meeting, a Request

Committee, chaired by the political affairs commissioner,was formed. It included the departments of Economy, Commerce, Justice and Agriculture. The purpose of this Request Committee was to handle all of the complaints formulated by both the Zairians and the European former owners who thought they were not compensated adequately.[34] This committee did not succeed because the acquisitors refused to cooperate and respond to the questionnaire submitted to them by the Request Committee.

During the entire period of Zairianization, there was no cooperation between the former European owners and the new Zairian acquisitors, nor were any compensation measures outlined for government reimbursement to the former owners. Few if any former European owners held key positions in the Zairianized businesses because, most of the acquisitors did not want to have any thing to do with the former owners, fearing that they would then need to share the wealth that they had just acquired.

Finally, in August 1974, President Mobutu admitted publicly, in the presence of all of the party leaders, commissioners and bureaucratic elites at the opening of the party school, the Makanda Kabobi Institute, that Zairianization had been a failure. President Mobutu stated that "with a few rare exceptions, and I insist on the word rare the manner in which the assignments and takeovers occurred is a veritable shame for most of the cadres of the MPR."[35] From then on, the acquisitors admitted that Zarianization measures had failed, and the ruling elites began taking measures that would return all the acquisitions to their former European, Zairian and MNC owners. These measures were termed "retrocession," and they became effective as of May 1977. The main losers of the Zairianization measures were

1. Zaire itself as a nation, because the measures helped widen the inequalities among classes and increased ethno-class conflicts;

2. the Europeans and the MNCs who became victims of the measures, lost all of their assets and had to start over after the retrocession measures;

3. the new ruling regime itself, which lost political influence at home and abroad.

The masses, leaders of opposition groups and the Western world began to doubt the seriousness of the regime, and sentiments of distrust built around the regime thereafter.

During the Second Republic, the new regime lost the trust of foreign investors and of the international institutions, such as the Paris Club, that had been their source of external support. These institutions became skeptical about the ability of the ruling elites to bring their politico-administrative machine to order.

The masses, as well as the Western institutions, began forcing the new ruling elites to come up with political, social and economic reforms that would help bring stability to the country and that would alleviate the anger and grievances of other ethnic groups, which were most neglected, such as the Lunda. Thus, in July 1977 (during the Second Republic), President Mobutu, for the first time after a long period, created the office of the prime minister.[36]   In order to stay in contact with a population (of which three-fourths lived in rural areas), a Ministry of Rural Development and the Office of Marketing Agricultural Produce were established. However, the actual importance of these new ministries and offices was insignificant, because all of the planning and major decisions remained in the hands of the president.

The most severe blow to the ruling elites and their Zairianization measures was the incursion of the Lunda ex-gendarmes Katangais and their exiled leaders to the copper-rich region of Shaba (Shaba I) in 1977. In 1978 the ex-gendarmes Katangais attempted once more to overthrow the regime (Shaba II).[37]   Political and economic stability are still far from being reached in Zaire due to the fact that the ruling elites still refuse to share any politico-administrative duties and responsibilities with the masses and the ethnic groups.

The main issues established so far show that the state-owned enterprises, mainly Gécamines, which provides 35 percent of Zaire's foreign exchange earnings, and other small enterprises, have failed in Zaire. This is a lesson for other developing countries of the world. The mining company, which is the cornerstone of Zaire's economy, was nationalized and Africanized. Management of this state-owned enterprise was taken over by political appointees who, for the most part, knew nothing about the industry. There was mismanagement and embezzlement of public funds, an official of the World Bank and the U.S. Agency for International Development said that "in 1988, about $400 million in revenues from Zaire's mineral exports disappeared and was never accounted for."[38]   Revenue generated from Gécamines was not being reinvested in other sectors of the economy.

In 1990 the government of Zaire government abandoned an economic recovery program devised by the International Monetary Fund.   Zaire's infrastructure and economy have collapsed, with the government unable to pay the salaries of civil servants and foreign creditors refusing any additional aid. The budget deficit helped push annual inflation rate from 1,000 percent in 1991[39] to 30,000 percent in 1992.[40]   Due to a sharp decrease in the availability of foreign exchange and the deficit spending, the national currency, the zaire, has depreciated rapidly against the American dollar. The zaire traded at about 300 zaires to the dollar in 1990, at about 19,000 zaires to the dollar in 1991 and in December 1992, it traded at 1,900,000 zaires to the dollar. Workers thoughout the big cities earn in a month the money needed to survive just three to four days.

The state-run hospitals in Zaire are closed for lack of medication and doctors have not been paid for years. Schools are closed, teachers have not been paid for months, "the banking system is near collapse and the capital, Kinshasa, is nearly without telephones, electricity or safe drinking water. People are limited to one meal a day."[41] In September 1991, about 3,000 Zairian paratroopers touched off widespread rioting and looting as they went on a rampage because the government had failed to pay them for months. This riot sparked a massive exodus of Zaire's expatriate community—a vital cog in the economy—and forced the closing of several small—and medium—businesses that were looted or wrecked by the hungry, frustrated populace.

This chapter has shown that many policy mistakes were made and that the result has been decay of Zaire's economy. The relevance of much of the material presented is that shows it how state-owned enterprises failed in Zaire. This is crucially important since over 85 percent of Zaire's foreign exchange earnings come from the state-owned enterprises, and the entire economy of Zaire depends on Gécamines. Gécamines is also Zaire's largest employer and the number one source of government revenues. Mismanagement and political problems continue to worsen the economic situation in Zaire. Government officials control the economy and discourage other citizens from entering the market. All the wealth is concentrated within the ruling elites and the embezzlement of state funds has been rampant in Zaire.

State-owned enterprises have failed to provide goods and services to the population in Zaire; they must be privatized. For the state-owned enterprises in Zaire, several of the forms of privatization discussed in Chapter 1 could be used: management privatization, sales of assets or equity, joint venture, liberalization or deregulation and contracting out. Since the public sector has been unable to deliver goods and services to consumers, the private sector should take over these responsibilities and restore transportation, communications and marketing functions that have virtually broken down since Zairianization. Law and order must be restored and reinforced and the system of property rights must also be restored.

The economic and political instability of Zaire was in free-fall well before the September 1991 riots. Because of the economic crisis and social and political turmoil, the opposition leaders pressed to have Zaire join the democratic trend sweeping much of Africa. A democratic conference was called in September 1991 with the goal to chart a path to democracy in Zaire. Zaire needs to follow the example of other developing countries that are promoting economic development and democracy through privatization because its state-owned enterprises, which are the cornerstone of Zaire's economy, have failed. Chapter 7 discusses the case of Cameroon and prospects for the success of privatization.

NOTES

1. Neil Henry, "France, Belgium Send Troops to Zaire," *Washington Post*, 25 September 1991, p. A19.
2. Janet MacGaffey, "Issues and Methods in the Study of African Economies," in *The Real Economy of Zaire*, ed. Janet MacGaffey (Philadelphia, Pennsylvania: University of Pennsylvania Press, 1991), 7.
3. Raymond Vernon, *The Promise of Privatization: A Challenge for U.S. Policy* (New York: Council on Foreign Relations Books, 1988), 219.
4. Ibid., 220.
5. Ibid.
6. "Update: Zaire," *Africa Report* 37 (July/August 1992): 12.

7. Ibid.

8. Interview with Michael Heydary, Foreign Minerals Specialist, U.S. Bureau of Mines Division of International Minerals, Washington, D.C., October 28,1992.

9. Neil Henry, "France, Belgium Send Troops to Zaire.

10. Sahr John Kpundeh, ed., *Democratization in Africa: Africa View, Africa Voices* (Washington, D.C.: National Research Council, National Academy Press, 1993), 38.

11. Richard L. Sklar, *Corporate Power in an African State* (Berkeley: University of California Press, 1975), 116.

12. "Mobutu's Empire of Graft," *Africa Now* 11 (March 1982): 12–23.

13. Interview with Nyangezi Kulimushi, Représentant de P.D.G. en Europe, SOZACOM, Brussels, February 11, 1983. Also interview with Jacques Leroy, Directeur Division Cuivre, Département Commercial Europe, SOZACOM, Brussels, February 11, 1983.

14. George W. Shepherd, *The Trampled Grass: Tributary States and Self-Reliance in the Indian Ocean Zone of Peace* (Wesport, Conn: Greenwood Press, 1987), 93.

15. Sklar, *Corporate Power*, 117.

16. Joseph LaPalombara and Stephen Blank, *Multinational Corporations and National Elites: A Study in Tensions* (New York: The Conference Board, Inc., 1976), 72.

17. Galen S. Hull, *Pawns on a Chess Board: The Resource War in Southern Africa* (Washington, D.C.: University Press of America, 1981), 31.

18. Zaire, Government Archives, *Labor Force in Katanga*, Document 21 (Lubumbashi: Zaire Government Publications, 1960), 21, Bustin, Edward, *Lunda under Belgian Rule: The Politics of Ethnicity* (Cambridge: Harvard University Press, 1975), 100–200.

19. Anthony Bouscaren, *Tshombe* (New York: Twin Circle Publishing, 1967), 14.

20. Mugur Valahu, *The Katanga Circus* (New York: Robert Speller & Sons, Inc., Publishers, 1964), 321.

21. "Forces in Zaire Open Fire on Democracy Demonstrators," *Washington Post,* 17 September 1992, p. A33.

22. "Les Mesures de Zairianisation," *JIWE* 3 (June 1974): 107–139.

23. Sklar, *Corporate Power*, 117.

24. Paul Collins, "The Political Economy of Indigenization: The Case of Nigerian Enterprises Promotion Decree," *African Review* 4 (1975): 491–508.

25. M. L. William, "The Extent and Significance of the Nationalization of Foreign-Owned Assets in Developing Countries, 1956–1972,"*Oxford Economic Paper* 27 (July 1975): 260–273.

26. Edward Kannyo, "Colonial Politics in Zaire 1960–1979," in *Zaire: The Political Economy of Underdevelopment*, ed. Guy Gran (New York: Praeger Publishers, 1979), 99.

27. Keith B. Richburg, "Economic Collapse Withers Lush Zaire," *Washington Post,* 31 March 1992, p. A1.

28. "Les Acquereurs," *Salongo,* 31 December 1973, p. 2.

29. Bustin, *Lunda Under Belgian Rule*, 137.

30. "Les Acquereurs et les Politiciens," *Salongo,* 2 January 1974, pp. 1–2.

31. "Discours du Président de la République à l'Occasion du Nouvel An,*Salongo,* 2 January 1974, pp. 1–4.

32. Michael G. Schatzberg, *Politics and Class in Zaire* (New York: Africana Publishing Company, 1980), 126.

33. "Les Entreprises d'Etat Ont échoué," *Salongo,* 30 July 1974, pp–5. Also Zaire Government Archives, *How State-Owned Enterprise Failed*, Doc. 36 (Kinshasa: Zaire Governement Publications, Department of Commerce, 1987), pp. 11–28.

34. "President Mobutu et son Discours sur les Acquereurs," *Salongo,* 25 March 1974, pp. 1–3.

35. "Discours du Président Fondateur du Mouvement Populaire de la Révolution à l'Ouverture de l'Institut Makanda Kabobi, le 5 Août 1974,"*Etudes Zairoises* 2 (June/July 1974): 205.

36. "Le Président a choisi son Premier Ministre," *Salongo,* 6 July 1977, pp. 1–2.

37. "The FNLC and the Regime," *Misonga* 3 (June 1978): 11–15.

38. Keith B. Richburg, "Mobutu: a Rich Man in Poor Standing,"*Washington Post,* 3 October 1991, p. A38.

39. Kenneth B. Noble, "Zaire Coalition Ends 26 Years of Dictatorship," *New York Times,* 30 September 1991, p. A6.

40. "Mr. Mobutu's Obligation to Zaire," *Washington Post*, 6 April 1992, p. A12.

41. Ibid.

The Case of Cameroon: Prospect for the Success of Privatization

ECONOMIC BACKGROUND OF CAMEROON

Throughout its first "quarter century, Cameroon has been one of African's few success stories."[1]   Cameroon has rich land, political stability, an industrious population and "enjoyed stable agriculture-led growth of 5 percent a year for nearly two decades following independence in 1960."[2]   From 1980 to 1986 with the discovery of oil, the growth rate accelerated to nearly 8 percent per year. Cameroon produced 7.7 million tons of petroleum in 1989. Two decades following independence, Cameroon followed "an admirable and well-documented path of economic growth and development."[3]

Before the discovery of oil, cash crops were Cameroon's principal export. Cameroon reinvested some of the funds derived from oil in the agricultural sector, which became its development priority.   Cameroon has a Western-oriented economy and it became a supplier of manufactured goods to central and west Africa "in addition to the long-standing export crops of timber, rubber, cotton, bananas, coffee and cocoa."[4]

Foreign investment through multinational corporations (Macs) has increased through the years due to an educated workhorse, a stable currency and a very good banking system as well as a dependable legal system. Thus foreign investment has played a major role in the economic growth of Cameroon. In 1980, of 100 largest enterprises in Cameroon, "foreign capital contributed 28.6 billion CFA francs or 48 percent of the total social capital of 59.6 billion CFA francs."[5]

In 1983, Cameroon's economy was growing at "6 percent in real terms giving a rate after inflation of over 3 percent per capita GAP."[6]   However in 1986, the prices of commodities in the world markets collapsed. This collapse put an end to the economic growth of Cameroon. The collapse in the prices of oil and cash crops helped the government of Cameroon reached a decision to privatize state-owned enterprises in the 1990s. The presence of 171 state-owned enterprises in Cameroon is not the cause of the increase in growth rate. The increase in growth rate was due to the discovery of oil.

However, before the collapse of the prices of commodities in the world markets, government officials were accused by opponents of "mismanagement and embezzlement of state funds."[7] There were too many state-owned enterprises mismanaged by political appointees who, in most cases, had no know-how in their industries. In the mid-1980s, international financial organizations, international donors and opponents of the regime began asking the government of Cameroon to privatize most of its state-owned enterprises. The 171 state-owned enterprises were becoming a burden and a cause of budgetary deficits. At that time, there was only one political party in Cameroon and there was no mass participation in decision making. The population demanded democratic reforms in the country.

The cause of Cameroon's economic malaise in the late 1980s was not only the decline of trade but also the mismanagement of state-owned enterprises and the embezzlement of state funds. The malaise could have been avoided if some of the enterprises had been privatized and others liquidated.

In 1988, the World Bank, the International Monetary Fund and bilateral donors, including the United States, France and Italy, as well as the African Development Bank provided Cameroon with loans designed to restore real per capita growth in the country. Based on past experience, the government of Cameroon knew that this growth could not be achieved through state-owned enterprises. State-owned enterprises had failed. Privatization of state-owned enterprises is the answer to promoting economic growth and building democratic infrastructure. Since there has been an economic crisis in Cameroon through the operation of state-owned enterprises, Cameroon decided to rely on privatization to achieve its goal of building build economic, social and political infrastructures.

Agriculture "employs the majority of Cameroonians (75 percent) and was responsible for two decades of stable growth through 1982."[8] Cameroon produces and exports the following food crops: bananas, beans, maize, manioc, paddy rice, pineapples, millet, sorghum, wheat, cocoa and coffee.

We have chosen the case of Cameroon and in particular the company Organization Camerounaise de la Banane (OCB), a newly privatized state-owned enterprise, to support our argument that privatization does bring about economic development and democracy. This case shows how privatization is actually working. Privatization promotes competition in the marketplace and improves efficiency and quality of goods and services at low cost to the maximization of consumer satisfaction. Since the privatization of OCB there has been an increase in income, and employees have participated in profit sharing. There is a sense of discipline and satisfaction among the employees with the management of the newly privatized company. Individuals are allowed to hold stocks. Proceeds are being injected into the local economy, and economic and democratic institutions are being built. The rate of growth of the economy is accelerating, and there is also an increase in the number of jobs being created.

Before privatization, the public sector in Cameroon, as in most of the developing countries, was the largest employer in the country. After privatizations, however, public-sector employees have been reduced significantly. The number of people working in the private sector has tremendously increased, especially in the agriculture sector. Since privatization started in Cameroon, "out of a total work force of 5,807,390, the total number of employees in the public sector amounts to 970,000 salaried and 200,000 civil servants. While in the private sector there are 4,368,580 employees."[9]

A Cameroonian official asserts that there has been "no tension between the multinational corporations (MNCs) who have acquired the newly privatized state-owned enterprises and the nationals due to many benefits and incentives that the MNCs are bringing to the country."[10]   This agrees with the opinion of Mark DeLancey who argues that Cameroon is a clear example of "a capitalist oriented state with foreign policy based on cooperation and interaction with the Western, capitalist countries of the world."[11]   There is, indeed, a strong relationship between the domestic economic system of Cameroon and the foreign policy of the nation, especially since the beginning of privatization.

State Ownership

Cameroon had 171 state-owned enterprises. The privatization process started in 1990. Out of fifteen state-owned enterprises that were selected to be privatized, six have already been privatized. Table 7.1 shows all fifteen of these state-owned enterprises, their capital, state-ownership, participation and the number of shares to be sold.

Table 7.1
State-Owned Enterprises to be Privatized
($US 1 = 292.11 FCFA)

Companies	Capital in 000 $US	State Ownership	Participation Shares to be Sold
Imprimerie Nationale	N.A.	100%	100%
Generale des Traveaux Metaliques (GETRAM)	5,688	100%	100%
Centre de Production et D'edition Pour l`Enseignement et la Recherche (CEPER)	N.A.	100%	100%
Société de Developpement de la Riziculture dans la Plaine des MBO (SODERIM)	N.A.	100%	100%

(Table 7.1, continued)

Office National de Developpement de L'agri culture et du Petit Betail (ONDAPB)	N.A.	100%	100%
Société Forestiere et Industrielle de Belabo (SOFIBEL)	6,511	79.43%	79.43%
Contreplaques du Cameroun (COCAM)	8,522	87.60%	87.60%
Ex Société des Crevettes du Cameroun en Liquidation Judiciaire	N.A.	N.A	N.A.
Cameroon Sugar Company (CAMSUCO)	4,404	98.12%	98.12%
Société Camerounaise de Metallurgie (SCDM)	5,049	86.82%	86.82%
Chocolaterie Confiserie Camerounaise (CHOCOCAM)	2,143	15.12%	15.12%
Société Camerounaise de Manutention d'acconage (SOCAMAC)	3,813	88.51%	88.51%
Société D'exploitation des Parcs a Bois du Cameroun (SEPBC)	942	35.00%	35.00%
Société D'equipement Pour L'afrique Cameroun (SEAC) en Liquidation Judiciaire	N.A.	N.A.	N.A.
Organisation Camerounaise de la Banane (OCB)	N.A.	100%	100%

Sources: This table compiled with the help of Privatization Document: Missions de Rehabilitation des Entreprises du Secteur Public et Para Public, Commission Technique, Economic and Trade Delegation (Washington, D.C.: Embassy of Cameroon, December 1992).

The privatization procedures designed by the government of Cameroon facilitated the privatization process and made it successful. These fifteen companies selected to be privatized can be classified into four groups:

Group A: Companies that have gone through the privatization process: (1) OCB, (2) SOCAMAC, (3) CHOCOCAM, (4) SCDM, (5) SEPBC;

Group B: Companies for sale by request of offers: (1) CAMSUCO, (2) SOFIBEL, (3) COCAM, and   (4) ONDAPB;

Group C: Companies that are just starting the privatization process: (1) GETRAM, (2) IMPRIMERIE NATIONALE, (3) CEPER, and (4) SODERIM;

Group D: Companies that are being legally liquidated: (1) SEAC, and (2) CREVCAM.

Like any other developing country, Cameroon inherited state-owned enterprises at the dawn of its independence. These state-owned enterprises have not been economically viable to serve as engines of development. The state acquired many more enterprises and subsidized them all.[12]

For three years, from 1986 to 1988, the economy of Cameroon suffered massively due to a rapid decrease in the price of its export commodities in the world markets. Budget deficits increased. Faced with this severe economic crisis, in 1989 the government of Cameroon adopted new economic measures, one of which was the privatization of state-owned enterprises. The World Bank, the International Monetary Fund and the African Development Bank approved loans under the terms of structural adjustment signed in 1989.

Privatization was the most important option adopted by the government as part of its economic stabilization program. The purpose of privatization was to promote the private sector, to increase productivity and competitiveness, to create jobs, to improve the quality of goods and services, to increase individual incomes and to allow individuals to own shares. All this would promote economic development and democracy.

The Move to Privatization

In order to implement privatization successfully, an interministerial committee was formed by Decree Law No. 86/656 of June 1989 which had a mission to oversee the entire privatization process. A technical commission was also formed by Decree Law No. 90/428 of February 1990 to oversee the technical ramifications of privatization.

Several Government officials have been sent abroad for training on privatization since 1990. A delegation of three key officials was sent to Washington, D.C., in November 1991 for a two-week training course on privatization at the International Development Training Institute.[13] The government also instituted a legal system to oversee the legality of privatization and in order to create a favorable investment climate for foreign companies and potential national and foreign individual investors. The government of Cameroon also outlined in detail all the principles, techniques and rules that would govern privatization operations in Cameroon.

The president of Cameroon, Paul Biya, signed decree laws that outline the rules and regulations to be followed in privatization process. Law No. 80/030, signed on December 29, 1989, authorizes privatization of state-owned enterprises. Decree Law No. 90/004 was signed on June 22, 1990, and Decree Law No. 90/1257 was signed on August 30, 1990. Decree Law No. 90/1425, which specifies the first enterprises to be privatized, was signed on October 3, 1990. Ordinance No. 90/7 of November 8, 1990, signed by the president of Cameroon stipulates that"all natural persons or corporate bodies of Cameroon or foreign nationality may, irrespective of their place of residence, undertake and engage in an economic activity in Cameroon."[14] The ordinance also states that "all natural persons or corporate bodies operating individually or in partnership shall, irrespective of the form taken in law by the economic activity, enjoy full protection under Cameroonian law."[15]   It stipulates that no expropriation, nationalization or requisition of a duly established undertaking or of its property shall be carried out without the state first initiating the procedure to declare such expropriation, "nationalization or requisition as being in the public interest and without prior compensation that is just equitable and based on a proper evaluation of the undertaking or of its property by an independent third party."[16]

These guarantees and others have opened the door to the foreign investments that are still pouring into Cameroon.   Many multinational corporations from the developed industrialized nations are investing in Cameroon.   Over fifteen of these have sent their offers to the government of Cameroon to purchase state-owned enterprises.   Socially and politically there are signs of stability in the country.

There is a multiparty system and presidential and parliamentary multiparty elections were held in the fall of 1992.   Since then everybody has been ready to go to work to help rebuild the country and continue the course of economic development and democracy.

The signs of political stabilization in Cameroon are not only the result of the multiparty elections in 1992, but also the result of participationof the masses in the decision-making process, lack of political turmoil, as is the case in Zaire, and respect for the rule of law.   Foreign investors are welcome in the country and feel at ease, and political unrest has decreased.   Entrepreneurs are able to conduct their international trade with the cooperation of local bankers and privatized enterprises.

Borders with neighboring countries are open, and the transportation and communication networks in the country are being restored with the cooperation of the MNCs that acquired state-owned enterprises.   All these are signs of stability. Ndongko states that "Cameroon's impressive political stability has also created an image that favours a particularly healthy business climate."[17]

Benefits and Advantages of Privatization in Cameroon

Multinational corporations and other national and foreign investors interested in purchasing state-owned enterprises through privatization enjoy the following benefits:

1. a 15 percent reduction rate covering custom duties, turnover tax and all other import duties payable on equipment, material for construction of the factory of the establishment, capital goods, machines and tools, rolling stock directly linked to the processes of production;

2. exemption from purchase tax on all goods when they are manufactured locally;

3. exemption from registration fees in respect of capital increases;

4. exemption from tax on the transfer of acquired premises, lands and buildings necessary for the implementation of the program and from the internal turnover tax or many other equivalent tax payable on studies, civil engineering works, the construction and installation of the buildings and equipment of the investment;

5. exemption from taxes on loans contracted in respect of investment program;
6. exemption from the minimum fixed tax payable as company tax;
7. exemption from the special company tax;
8. a 50 percent reduction of company tax for the first year;
9. a 50 percent reduction for corporate bodies, industrial and commercial profits, and a 50 percent reduction of proportional tax levied on the income of movable assets.[18]

Ordinance No. 90/7 also requires the acquisitors of the newly privatized state-owned enterprises to create permanent jobs for Cameroonians. The natural resources and/or goods and services produced in Cameroon must equal 50 percent of the value of inputs. They must have a production for export equal to at least 50 percent of annual turnover exclusive of taxes. All these benefits are designed to promote economic growth and development, meet the basic needs of the population and build economic, social and political infrastructures in Cameroon. This proves our point that privatization promotes economic development and democracy in the developing countries.

Privatization at Work: The Case of Organization Camerounaise de la Banane (OCB)

Having put all these privatization procedures in place, in October 1991 the government of Cameroon selected fifteen enterprises to be privatized. Table 7.1 shows these first fifteen selected enterprises. These firms represented all sectors of the economy of Cameroon from Agribusiness, the steel industry, printing, the tool industry, the food industry and transportation. Among these companies, six have been sold. Among the successfully privatized companies, l'Organisation Camerounaise de la Banane ranks number one. OCB became Société des Bananeries de la Mbome (SBM) when privatized. We come back to this later in the chapter.

Buyers or Acquisitors

Who are the buyers or acquisitors of these privatized state-owned enterprises in Cameroon? Due to the lack of a capital market in the country and the lack of buying power among the nationals, almost all the stockholders of the newly privatized state-owned enterprises in Cameroon are multinational corporations and private investors from the developed industrialized countries. Has there been any tension between the MNCs, foreign investors and the population due to the fact that all the newly privatized companies are owned by foreign investors? We did not find this to be the case. There is a strong working relationship between the MNCs, the population and the government of Cameroon. MNCs and foreign private investors are setting aside a certain number of shares to be purchased by the employees of the newly privatized firms.

The incomes of the employees of the newly privatized state-owned enterprises are higher under the MNC management than those earned under state management.

The society in general is pleased with the benefits derived from these newly privatized state-owned enterprises: employment is gaining and increasing, incomes are higher, the standard of living of the employees and their dependents is increasing, funds are being reinvested in schools, hospitals, small and medium enterprises and new jobs are being created in related industries.[19] This concurs with the point made by Ndongko that "the doctrine of social justice aims at redistributing the fruit of development equitably among different groups and giving each citizen an equal opportunity within the framework of material solidarity."[20]

There is also participation of the masses in the process. Democratic institutions are being built. There is a multiparty system in 1991–92 for the first time since independence. People begin to see that they really have a stake in the newly privatized enterprises. There are signs of economic and political stability. People freely participated in the general elections held in the fall of 1992. This is what we have been arguing and what privatization is supposed to bring: the conditions for economic development and democracy. Privatization does promote economic development and democracy.

With the success of the few newly privatized state-owned enterprises and in particular that of the Organization Camerounaise de la Banane, the government of Cameroon should continue to aggressively pursue this process of privatization with the remaining bulk of state-owned enterprises. They have become a burden to the state. They must be privatized. At the same time the benefits instituted by the government create a very attractive investment climate for foreign investors participating in this process privatization process. These measures and benefits are designed to satisfy both the host country and foreign investors. Any dispute is settled in due course in a court of law. Other developing countries that are planning to privatized state-owned enterprises should follow this example.

We have chosen the company OCB because it is "the most successful case of privatization, so far among all the newly privatized state-owned enterprises in Cameroon."[21] The quality of goods and services produced by this newly privatized state-owned enterprise "has increased so tremendously that it is creating new jobs. There has been an increase in income, employees are participating in profit sharing, and individuals are allowed to hold stocks in this newly privatized company."[22] As a matter of fact, André Blaise Kesseng states, "the export earnings of this newly privatized company have skyrocketed and the quality of the goods produced by O.C.B has improved so drastically that it has become the envy of its competitors."[23] No specific problems have cropped up among the other privatizations. Privatization of the banana industry is the most successful for the reasons mentioned here. Before Organization Camerounaise de la Banane was privatized, the quality of the bananas it produced ranked number two and number three in the world market. After privatization, the newly privatized company, Société de Bananeries de Mbome improved the quality of its banana from numbers two and three to number one.[24] Before SBM took over this state-owned enterprise, the quality of the bananas its produced ranked also third, that is, after the cocoa, cotton and wood industries. The newly privatized state-owned enterprise, Société de Bananeries de la Mbome is a modern agri-business industry with up-to-date equipment and best management style. It does not buy any bananas from farmers. It grows its own bananas, and the quality of its fruits has been accepted in the international market.

In Cameroon as well as in other developing countries, "governments have started using the proceeds derived from privatization of state-owned enterprises and are injecting these funds in domestic programs specifically targeted to help build economic and democratic infrastructures, with the single purpose of promoting economic development and democracy."[25]

Employees of the Organization Camerounaise de la Banane are working much harder than when the company was a state-owned enterprise because the working conditions provided by the new management have improved, and the incentives derived from the fruit of their labor have increased. They are allowed to purchase stocks and participate in profit sharing. As efficiency, performance and competition increase, the quality of goods and services improve and the financial performance of this newly privatized enterprise also improve. The employees are awarded more benefits and profit sharing increases. André Blaise Kesseng argues that "there is no doubt that the private sector, and specifically the newly privatized enterprises, are accelerating the rate of growth of the economy of Cameroon."[26]

In Cameroon as well as in Mali the government and the private sector are working hand in hand to "speed up the privatization process in all developing countries due to the benefits derived from privatization as proven by some success stories of privatization."[27]

The privatization of the state-owned enterprise Organization Camerounaise de la Banane was done in a classic scenario, and it was conducted as follows: evaluation, request for offers, negotiation and signature of protocol of agreement and of the convention of relinquishment.[28]

Evaluation

Independent evaluations of OCB were conducted by three companies: Closse/PROPARCO (CCCE) in May 1988, KOOH et MURE in August 1989 and Arthur Anderson in 1989. In October 1990, the subcommittee in charge of privatization went over all the evaluation procedures and methodology.

Request for Offers: Potential Buyers

On October 13, 1990, the government called for requests for offers at the national and international levels. The government of Cameroon emphasized that all the offers must be in by November 15, 1990. On this date, three offers were received by the subcommittee in charge of privatization. These offers came from the following multinational corporations:

1. Groupe Terres Rouges Consultant,
2. Groupe Pomona et Laugier Gillot et Cie;
3. Groupe Compagnie Fruitière.

After analyzing and scrutinizing these three offers, the selection of the best offer to acquire the company OCB was based on the following criteria:

1. the purchasing price;
2. the amount of investment;
3. number of employees to be safeguarded or protected;
4. benefits solicited.

On November 22, 1990, the interministerial commission retained the offer from Groupe Compagnie Fruitière, a French agri-business multinational corporation.

Multinational corporations were able to purchase state-owned enterprises in Cameroon because they had the capital. Ndongko argues that opportunities for local businessmen to "accumulate capital and lead this country along the path of independent industrialization are not simply present."[29] The cause often emphasized is that the structure of the economy after independence "continues the patterns of the colonial state in placing constraints on the development of an indigenous class of capitalists."[30]

Negotiations

The negotiations between the government and Groupe Compagnie Fruitière, a French MNC, took place in November and December 1990 and concluded with an amelioration of the initial offer based on the following:[31]

1. value of assets;
2. investment plan;
3. salaries of personnel;
4. accompanying measures.

Based on these factors, a protocol of agreement was signed on December 20, 1990 between the government and Groupe Compagnie Fruitière. The document of transfer of ownership was signed on February 15, 1991, at which point Organization Camerounaise de la Banane was acquired by the French agri-business conglomerate Groupe Compagnie Fruitière / France. The newly privatized company is Société des Bananeries de la Mbome. It is an agribusiness industry specializing in the production and export of bananas. Banana production has become the number one sector of the agriculture in Cameroon. As a matter of fact, the newly privatized company SBM has become a strategic firm in Cameroon.[32]

The convention of establishment between Cameroon and Société de Bananeries de la Mbome of Groupe Compagnie Frutière / France was signed on March 10, 1992. The SBM has been included among the strategic industries by the government of Cameroon because it brings more foreign exchange to the country than any other newly privatized enterprise.[33] Hence, SBM has all the advantages provided in the Investment Code in order to increase its competitiveness in the world markets. This was accomplished in less than two years.

Productivity, Competitiveness and Export Earnings of SBM

As mentioned earlier the production of bananas is the first sector of the agriculture of Cameroon. Table 7.2 shows banana exports for 1986–87 and 1987–88. As Table 7.2 shows, SBM export for 1992–93 is estimated to be 220,000 metric tons,[34] whereas that of 1987-88, when the enterprise was state owned, was only 40,320 metric tons. The increase in production is due to the benefits and incentives provided to the employees.

Table 7.2
Douala Port Traffic
(metric tons)

Export	1986–87	1987–88
Bananas	50,359	40,320

Source: Ministry of Commerce, Yaounde, Cameroon.

Table 7.3
SBM Export
(metric tons)

Estimated export	1992–93
Bananas	220,000

Source: Document, Economic and Trade Delegation, (Washington, D.C.: Embassy of Cameroon, December 1992), p. 6.

Here we clearly see the result of privatization. There has been increase in production. When the company was under state ownership, the production was low and there was no competition. The quality of goods and services was poor and the income generated by the workers and the state was low. After this banana company was privatized, the production increased more than 500 percent. For

1992–93 Société des Bananeries de la Mbome has become the number one foreign exchange earner in the entire agricultural sector in Cameroon. SBM export for 1992-93 are valued at 40 milliard FCFA [35] or $US 0.14 billion (see Table 7.4). Under state ownership, however, the enterprises' foreign exchange earnings were almost nonexistent due to the lack of employee incentives and the poor quality of the bananas produced.

Table 7.4
SBM Export Earnings

Year	Amount
1992–93	40 milliard FCFA or $US 0.14 billion

Source: Document, Economic and Trade Delegation, (Washington, D.C.: Embassy of Cameroon, December 1992).

Along with the exponential increase in production and export earnings, there has been also an increase in income for employees with a very noticeable increase in new jobs for Cameroonians since the privatization of this company. Some of the profits generated from sales are being reinvested in the local economy, helping to build schools, hospitals and roads. Employees are participating in the decision making of the company since they have a stake in it. They are, for the first time, allowed to purchase stocks. They also participate in profit sharing. Economic and democratic infrastructures are being built. The government has already planned to reinvest revenues derived from privatization in the local economy to stimulate growth.[36]

This case of the privatization of a state-owned enterprise clearly establishes the fact that privatization promotes economic development and democracy. The evidence presented in this chapter concerning privatization of the banana company Organization Camerounaise de la Banane in Cameroon presents a stark contrast to the failure of state-owned enterprises in Zaire. All efforts must be exerted by the governments of developing countries to privatize their state-owned enterprises.

NOTES

1. *Marketing in Cameroon, Overseas Business Report* (Washington, D.C.: U.S. Department of Commerce, International Trade Administration, September 1990), 3.
2. Ibid.
3. Alfred A. Ndongko, "The Political Economy of Development in Cameroon: Relations between the State, Indigenous Business, and Foreign Investors," in *The Political Economy of Cameroon,* eds., Michael G. Schatzberg and I. William Zartman (New York: Praeger, 1986), 83.
4. *Marketing in Cameroon, Overseas Business Report,* 3.

5. Ndongko, "The Political Economy of Development in Cameroon," 92.

6. Ibid., 83.

7. For more information, see, interview with John Fru Ndi by Jean-Baptiste Placca, "Cameroon, John Fru Ndi En Campagne," *Jeune Afrique* 159 (September 1992): 124.

8. *Marketing in Cameroon, Overseas Business Report,* 8.

9. Celestin Monga, "50 propositions Pour Sauver l'Economie du Cameroon," *Jeune Afrique* 159 (September 1992): 114.

10. Interview with André Blaise Kesseng, Economic Counselor, Embassy of Cameroon, Washington, D.C., December 7, 1992.

11. Mark W. DeLancey, " Cameroon's Foreign Relations," in *The Political Economy of Cameroon*, eds. Michael G. Schatzberg and I. William Zartman (New York: Praeger, 1986), 189.

12. *Document de la Sous Commission de Privatisation des Entreprises*, Bureau du Premier Ministre, Yaounde, Cameroon, February 1994.

13. This delegation was composed of Roger Mbassa Ndine, President CT/MREP; Vincent Mendounga Akenga, Ministry of Planning; Evarist Ngaba, Sub-Commission on Privatization, government of Cameroon.

14. Ordinance No. 90/7 of November 8, 1990 to Institute the Investment Code of Cameroon, 1. Economic and Trade Delegation, Embassy of Cameroon, Washington, D.C., December 17, 1992.

15. Ibid.

16. Ibid., 2.

17. Afred A. Ndongko, "The Political Economy of Development in Cameroon," 83.

18. Ordinance No. 90/7 of November 1990 to Institute the Investment Code of Cameroon, 6. Economic and Trade Delegation, Embassy of Cameroon, Washington, D.C., December 17, 1992.

19. For more information, see, Cameroon, *Document: Société de Bananeries de la Mbome (S.B.M.)*, 5–10, Muntengume, Cameroon, May 1993. Also Staff Writer, "Etat d'Avancement du Premier Programme de Privatisation," *Document 2*—Mission de Rehabilitation des Entreprises du Secteur Piblic et Para Public (Yaounde, Cameroon: Commission Technique, 1993), 5–7.

20. Ndongko, "The Political Economy of Development in Cameroon," 102.

21. Interview with André Blaise Kesseng, Economic Counselor, Embassy of Cameroon, Washington, D.C., December 7, 1992.

22. Ibid.

23. Ibid. Also "Etat d'Avancement du Premier Programme de Privatisation," 5–7.

24. See, Cameroon, *Documents: Société de Bananeries de la Mbome (S.B.M.),* Economic and Trade Delegation of Cameroon, Washington, D.C.: Embassy of Cameroon, May 1993. Also *Document de la Sous Commission de Privatisation des Entreprises*, Yaounde, Cameroon: Bureau du Premier Ministre, February 1994.

26. Interview with Ousmane Sedibé, Director, Agency For Promotion of Private Enterprise, Government of Mali, Washington, D.C., July 16, 1992.

27. Interview with André Blaise Kesseng, Economic Counselor, Embassy of Cameroon, Washington, D.C., December 7, 1992.

28. Interview with Bakary Diarra, Director, Office of Public Sector, Government of Mali, Washington, D.C., July 16, 1992.

29. "Etat d'Avancement du Premier Programme de Privatization," *Document - Mission de Rehabilitation des Entreprises du Secteur Public et Para Public* (Yaounde, Cameroon: Commission Technique, 1992), 3–4.

30. Ndongko, "The Political Economy of Development in Cameroon, 94.

31. Ibid., 94.

32. Cameroon, *Privatization of Organization Camerounaise de la Banane (O.C.B.),* Economic and Trade Delegation, (Washington, D.C.: Embassy of Cameroon, December 1992).

33. Ibid., 5.

34. Cameroon, *Document: Société de Bananeries de la Mbome (S.B.M.),* (Yaounde, Cameroon: Minister of Commerce, March 1993), 5.

35. Cameroon, *Document, Société des Bananeries de la Mbome (S.B.M.),* Economic and Trade Delegation, (Washington, D.C.: Embassy of Cameroon, December 1992), 5.

36. Ibid.

37. Cameroon, *Document de la Sous Commission de Privatisation des Entreprises* (Yaounde, Cameroon: Bureau du Premier Ministre, February 1994). Also Staff Writer, "Stabilisation et Relance Economique: Privatisation des Entreprises," *Cameroon Tribune* 6 (December 1993): 6–12.

Conclusions: Who is to Gain from Privatization, the Western World or the Developing Countries?

Who is to gain from privatization in the developing countries, the Western world or the developing countries? This is a very complex question and deserves a good answer. It was argued earlier that the aim of privatization is to reduce the role that the government plays in national economies and to encourage the private sector to take over this role. Politics plays the most important role in deciding whether or not to privatize. Privatization is the best means to enhance efficiency by stimulating competition. We commonly view privatization as a process of transferring assets from the public sector to the private sector. We discussed privatization and its various forms: sales of assets, contracting out, subsidies, liberalization or deregulation, management privatization and so forth.

Throughout this study we have seen that most state-owned enterprises are losing money. The case of Gécamines thoroughly documented this point. We have discussed cases of mismanagement, gross incompetence, looting and embezzlement of funds from the state-owned enterprises. It is clear that the governments of developing countries have failed to reach their goals of promoting economic development and growth through the operation of state-owned enterprises. We defined economic development as a process in which there is growth in the nation's economy, where there is sustained improvement in the well-being of the people, where there is a rise in gross national product (GNP); a process where the gap between the rich and the poor decreases over time; a process where the entrepreneurs play a key role in the economic growth of a nation, and where the private sector dominates the economy of the country.

In almost all the developing countries where the private sector is very limited and where state-owned enterprises dominate the nation's economy, there has been no economic development, as measured by the gross national product. This is the case especially in the poorer Sub-Saharan African countries where economies have become worse than they were before independence. Economic development takes place when there is an increase in GNP per capita over time.

Privatization of state-owned enterprises would help reach this goal. We have seen very few developing countries where economic development is taking place: South Korea, Hong Kong, Singapore, Argentina, Brazil and in Sub-Saharan Africa, Côte D'Ivoire and in particular Cameroon, due mainly to privatization efforts and the policy of free enterprise adopted by their governments. Rapid economic growth has resulted in those developing countries where the governments have given freedom to individuals and the private sector to pursue their enterprises. This has benefited the entire society.

As we have seen in the case of Cameroon, privatization does promote economic development and democracy. Competition has increased. The quality of goods and services in the privatized enterprise has improved, production has increased tremendously, export earnings have skyrocketed, new jobs are being created and incomes have increased. Employees are participating in profit sharing, and individuals are allowed to purchase stocks in the newly privatized enterprise. Proceeds derived from privatization are being used by the government and are being reinvested in domestic programs, building economic and democratic infrastructures. The governments of the developing countries must give free reign to innovators, entrepreneurs motivated by Adam Smith's invisible hand. This will promote competition and efficiency and produce goods and services that meet the demands of consumers and generate economic growth.

So, who is to benefit by privatization? It is obvious from this analysis that the developing countries will benefit from privatization. And those developing countries that have successfully privatized state-owned enterprises are already benefiting from privatization. We would say also that the Western world, multinational corporations and foreign investors will benefit greatly from privatization of strategic state-owned enterprises.

In the case of investment by Westerns and multinational corporations in the privatization of strategic industries such as mining (goal, diamonds, cobalt, copper, silver, uranium, etc.), crude oil and coffee, these Western investors would gain substantially. They have the technology, especially since these industries are capital and technology intensive. They have the markets, since most of these commodities and cash crops are marketed in the industrialized developed countries where the prices are controlled by the Western investors. Finally, they have the know-how and hold the patents on all equipment and machinery used in the extraction and exploitation of minerals and also in the crude oil industry.

It is a fact that privatization of state-owned enterprises in Sub-Saharan Africa, Asia and Latin America will not succeed unless the Western industrialized developed countries, international financial institutions, such as the World Bank and the International Monetary Fund (IMF), and other aid donors continue to put pressure on these governments to privatize the public sector and, most important, that these Western nations and international financial institutions continue to make financial resources available to those developing countries that are honestly and truly following the path of privatization in its various forms, as discussed in this study.

Once the spirit of free enterprise reigns in these developing countries through privatization, the free market economy and democracy will emerge, as we have seen in the case of successful privatization in Cameroon. There is a relationship between capitalism and democracy, as argued earlier. Adam Smith sees capitalism clearly as an adjunct to good life and human freedom. The people in the developing countries want good life and want their basic human needs met, and the Western world and international financial institutions should provide the financial resources to help implement a capital market infrastructure in the developing countries. Western assistance would facilitate the privatization process and encourage free enterprise. It would also provide goods and services to meet the demands of the consumer. Failure to do so by the Western countries will see a massive exodus of immigrants from the developing countries of Africa, Asia and Latin America to North America, Europe and Japan; the example of Haiti is a case in point. That would have severe consequences on the standard of living enjoyed by the people in the Western world and would result in major political problems worldwide.

The World Bank and the IMF must continue, at all costs, to assist the developing countries with economic reforms that will help eliminate mismanagement, which has been one of the reasons for economic decline in the developing countries. The IMF, with structural adjustment and its enhanced structural adjustment facilities, must continue to help these poor developing countries in order to foster economic growth. The governments of the developing countries must refrain from intervening in the private sector. The promising avenue for these developing countries is to sell the assets of state-owned enterprises to the private sector.

Developing countries have much to gain by privatizing their state-owned enterprises; namely, mismanagement and embezzlement would be reduced, there would be competition and efficiency in the private sectors, the best quality of goods and services would be available, payment problems would be solved and measures to improve their balance-of-payments would be implemented. And eventually, developing countries with export-oriented industries will be able to compete in the world market. The private sector is to provide the goods and services to meet the demands of the consumers and not the public sector.

The governments of the developing countries have been running large deficits caused by the financial borrowing by the state-owned enterprises at home and abroad. These state-owned enterprises have become a constraint on economic development and on the distribution of wealth and income. Therefore, these developing countries will gain tremendously by privatizing their enterprises. As argued earlier, these state-owned enterprises have failed due to the lack of managerial skills and know-how since most of the staff are political appointees who lack expertise in the fields where they are appointed. Inefficiencies, poor performance, low quality of goods and services, misallocation of resources and lack of managerial skill are the causes of budgetary burdens for the state-owned enterprises. Hence, the governments of the developing countries have everything to gain by privatizing their state-owned enterprises. Privatization is a means to eradicate poverty, to increase income, to promote competition and to better the quality of goods and services for the population.

These developing countries need help from the Western countries in developing capital markets in order to expand the private sector and give every individual an equal opportunity to participate. Because, in most cases, only ethnic minority and government elites, who make up disproportionate numbers of potential domestic buyers of public assets, are gaining from privatization. The multinational corporations that have shown interest in participating in the purchase of assets have quite often aligned themselves with the government elites and ethnic ruling minority so that the society as a whole has yet to benefit from privatization. However, in a few countries, such as Argentina, Brazil, Cameroon, Côte d'Ivoire, Hong Kong, Singapore and South Korea, the multinational corporations and foreign private investors that have acquired the newly privatized state-owned enterprises have allowed employees to purchase stock and to participate in profit sharing. In these cases, the population as a whole is benefiting from privatization.

In participating in privatization in the developing countries, the MNCs have plenty to gain. Not only would they maximize their profits by finding new markets for their products, they would also bring awareness of their products to different people, territories and countries and obtain raw materials for their industries. The MNCs and foreign private investors will also make an economic contribution to the host countries, build a technological infrastructure, promote economic growth and improve the standard of living of the people. The host countries, through foreign direct investment from the MNCs, will start developing the badly needed market economy that is the engine of economic development and democracy around the world. Foreign direct investment can aid economic development when it contributes more to the income of the host country. And foreign direct investment, especially in manufacturing and extraction, is believed to be an effective means to achieve industrialization. It also helps the augmentation of capital formation and transplantation of technological knowledge. Foreign direct investment is considered the best way of obtaining external funds.

Therefore, the developing countries of Africa, Asia and Latin America must bring about a fundamental transformation of their existing institutional structures and state-owned enterprises in order to promote economic development and growth. As we have seen so far, the MNCs and foreign private investors from the Western industrialized nations and the developing countries themselves will both gain from privatization of state-owned enterprises in the developing countries.

However, we should caution that despite the huge gains by the developing countries that could derive from privatization, huge state-owned enterprise sectors will remain due to many reasons we have discussed earlier—among them, political risks by the minority ruling ethnic group elites that hold power and monopoly and control in these enterprises and who are not ready to relinquish them. Hence, international financial institutions and the Western donors should seriously consider assisting small and medium free enterprises in the developing countries as well as promoting new enterprises in these nations.

If privatization is to be successful in the developing countries, international financial institutions, such as the World Bank and the IMF, the Western industrialized nation donors and the MNCs must, through foreign direct investments, continue the flow of financial resources to better help the transition from public sector to private sector development.

Who is to gain from privatization in the developing countries? Figure 8.1 shows who is to gain in the short and long terms. It shows that both developed and developing countries are going to benefit from privatization. However, in the developing countries, there are mainly two groups that will benefit from privatization in the short and long terms: the ruling elites and government officials, on one hand, and the population as a whole, on the other. The privatized firms creat new jobs. The quality of goods and services produced in the newly privatized enterprises have improved at competitive prices, and export earnings have skyrocketed. The group that will gain the most from privatization in the developing countries is the developed industrialized nations, specifically, the MNCs and the private investors. They have huge capital to purchase the state-owned enterprises to be privatized, and they usually associate themselves with the government officials and the ruling elites who become, in most cases, their associates in business. The MNCs and private investors in the developed countries have at their disposal a sophisticated information and communication networks, know-how, management skills, high technology, easy access to the world markets and all the necessary tools needed to improve the quality of goods and services to be produced in the newly privatized enterprises, which makes the competition keen.

The MNCs and other foreign investors are responding to the economic turnaround and to the opportunities presented by the government privatization programs in a few developing countries. These foreign investors and MNCs have produced an inflow of private capital in the developing countries. Proceeds and tax revenues derived from privatization rose during 1991 and 1992. The governments of developing countries where the privatization process has been successful have been reinvesting revenues in domestic programs. Many developing countries' economies were staggering under hyperinflation, a bloated and inefficient public sector and a huge fiscal deficit. There has been a turnaround in a few of those countries as a result of successful government privatization programs coupled with persistent government efforts to reform their economies and eliminate macroeconomic imbalance.

Privatization of state-owned enterprises has reduced government spending, import controls and tariffs. It has encouraged competition and national and foreign private investment. Privatization has fostered economic growth and development and is building solid economic and democratic infrastructures. The population is participating in the privatization process, and the society as a whole is benefiting from privatization.

Figure 8.1
Privatization

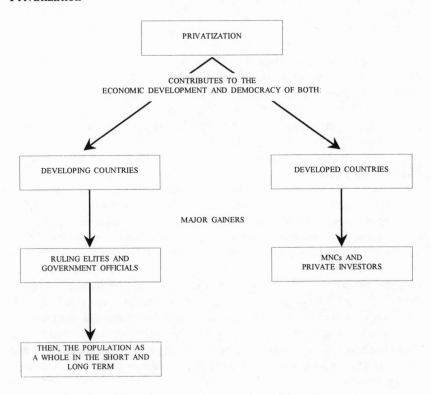

We highly recommend that privatization programs be designed and carried out in all developing countries on a case-by-case basis, and that training programs be set up to train government officials, academic and international institutions and international donors as to how to privatize state-owned enterprises in the developing countries.

Bibliography

Adhikari, Ramesh, and Colin Kirkpatrick. "Public Enterprise in Less Developing Countries: An Empirical Review." In *Public Enterprise at the Crossroads: Essays in Honour of V. V. Ramanadham,* edited by John Heath, 24–43. New York: Routledge, 1990.

Adler, John H., ed. *Capital Movement and the Economic Development.* New York: St. Martin's Press, 1967.

Aharoni, Yair. "The United Kingdom: Transforming Attitudes." In *The Promise of Privatization: A Challenge for U.S. Foreign Policy,* edited by Raymond Vernon, 27. New York: Council on Foreign Relations Books, 1988.

Amin, Samir. "Peace, National and Regional Security and Development: Some Reflections on the African Experience." In *Breaking the Link: Development Theory and Practice in Southern Africa,* edited by Robert Mazur, Trenton, N.J.: Africa World Press, 1990.

Amin, Samir, and Carl Widstrand. *Multinational Firms in Africa.* Upsala: Scandinavian Institute of African Studies and the African Institute for Economic Development and Planning, 1975.

Austin, James E. *Managing in Developing Countries: Strategic Analysis and Operating Techniques.* New York: Free Press, 1990.

Averch, Harvey. *Private Markets and Public Intervention: A Primer for Policy Designers.* Pittsburgh, Penn.: University of Pittsburgh Press, 1990.

Ayittey, George B. N. "How Africa Ruined Itself." *The Wall Street Journal* (December 9, 1992), p.1.

Ayub, M. S., and S. O. Hegstad. "Management of Public Industrial Enterprises." *World Bank Research Observers* 2 (1987): 79–101.

Babai, Don. "The World Bank and the IMF: Rolling Back the State or Backing its Role?" In *The Promise of Privatization: A Challenge for U.S. Policy,* edited by Raymond Vernon, 254–273. New York: Council on Foreign Relations Books, 1988.

Balassa, Bella. *Economic Progress, Private Value and Public Policy, Essays in Honor of William Felener.* New York: Balassa and Nelson, 1977.

Baldwin, Robert E., and Gerald M Meier. *Economic Development: Theory, History, Policy*. New York: John Wiley & Sons, 1957.

Baran, Paul A., and Paul M. Sweezy. "Notes on the Theory of Imperialism." In *Problems and Economic Dynamics and Planning: Essays in Honor of Michal Kalecki*, 20. Warsaw: Polish Scientific Publishers, 1964.

Baum, W. C., and S. M.Tolbert. *Investing in Development: Lessons of World Bank Experience*. Oxford: Oxford University Press for the World Bank, 1985.

Bendick, Marc, Jr. "Privatizing the Delivery of Social Welfare Services: An Idea to be Taken Seriously." In *Privatization and The Welfare State*, edited by Alfred J. Kahn and Sheila B. Kamerman, 98, Princeton, N.J.: Princeton University Press, 1989.

Berg, Elliot. "The Role of Diverstiture in Economic Growth." In *Privatization and Development*, edited by Steve H. Hanke, 23. San Francisco, Calif.: International Center for Economic Growth Press, 1987.

Berg Report. *Accelerated Development in Sub-Saharan Africa*. Washington, D.C.: The World Bank, 1981.

Berger, Peter L., and Richard John Neuhaus. *To Empower People: The Role of Mediating Structures in Public Policy*. Washington, D.C.: American Enterprise Institute, 1977.

Beuber, Grant L. *Private Foreign Investment in Development*. Oxford: Clarendon Press, 1973.

Blank, Stephen, and Joseph LaPalombara. *Multinational Corporations and National Elites: A Study in Tensions*. New York: The Conference Board, 1976.

Blejer, Mario, and Vito Tanzi. "Fiscal Deficits and Balance of Payments Desequilibrium in IMF Adjustment Programs." In *Adjustment, Conditionality and International Financing*, edited by Joaquin Muns, 117–136. Washington, D.C.: International Monetary Fund, 1984.

Blejer, Mario I., and Mohsin S. Khan. "Government Policy and Private Investment in Developing Countries." Washington, D.C.: International Monetary Fund, Staff Papers Vol. 31, 379–403, June, 1984.

Bouscaren, Anthony. *Tshombe*. New York: Twin Circle Publishing, 1967.

Brett, E. A. "States, Markets and Private Power: Problems and Possibilities." In *Privatization in Less Developed Countries*, edited by Paul Cook and Colin Kirkpatrick, 58. New York: St. Martin's Press, 1988.

Brodkin, Evelyn Z., and Dennis Young. "Making Sense of Privatization: What Can We Learn from Economic and Political Analysis?" In *Privatization and the Welfare State*, edited by Alfred J. Kahn and Sheila B. Kamerman, 123. Princeton, N.J.: Princeton University Press, 1989.

Brooke, Michael Z., and Lee Remmers, eds. "Organization and Finance." In *The Strategy of Multinational Enterprise*. London: Longman, 1970.

Bustin, Edouard. *Luanda under Belgium Rule: The Politics of Ethnicity*. Cambridge, Mass.: Harvard University Press, 1975.

Butler, Stuart M. *Privatizing Federal Spending: A Strategy to Eliminate the Deficit*. New York: Universe Books, 1985.

——. "Privatization for Public Purposes." In *Privatization and the Welfare State*, edited by Alfred J. Kahn and Sheila B. Kamerman, 17–24. Princeton, N.J.: Princeton University Press, 1989.

Callaghy, Thomas M., and Ernest J. Wilson III. "Africa: Policy, Reality or Rituals?" In *The Promise of Privatization: A Challenge to U.S. Policy*, edited by Raymond Vernon, 180. New York: Council on Foreign Relations Books, 1988.

Cameroon. *Document de la Sous Commission de Privatisation des Entreprises*. Yaounde: Cameroon, Bureau du Premier Ministre, February 1994.

Cameroon. *Document sur la Société de Bananerie de la Mbome (S.B.M.)*, p. 5. Yaounde: Minister of Commerce, March 1993.

Cameroon. *Document: Société de Bananerie de la Mbome. (S.B.M.)*. Economic and Trade Delegation of Cameroon. Washington, D.C.: Embassy of Cameroon, May 1993.

Cameroon. *Documents: Société de Bananeries de la Mbome (S.B.M.)*, 5–10. Muntengume: Cameroon, May 1993.

Cameroon. *Ordinance No. 90/7 of 8 November 1990 to Institute the Investment Code of Cameroon*. Economic and Trade Delegation. Washington, D.C.: Embassy of Cameroon, December 17, 1992.

Cameroon. *Privatization of Organisation Camerounaise de la Banane (O.C.B.)*. Economic and Trade Delegation of Cameroon. Washington, D.C.: Embassy of Cameroon, December 1992.

Campbell, R. H., A. Smith, and W. B. Todd, eds. *An Inquiry into the Causes of the Wealth of Nations*. London: Liberty Classics, 1976.

Caves, Richard E. "Industrial Organization." In *Economic Analysis and the Multinational Enterprise*, edited by John Dunning, 21. New York: Praeger, 1974.

Cheetham, Russell J., Allen C. Kelley and Jeffrey G. Williamson. *Dualistic Economic Development. Theory and History*. Chicago: The University of Chicago Press, 1972.

Collins, Paul. "The Political Economy of Indigenization: The Case of Nigerian Enterprises Promotion Decree." *African Review* 4(1975): 491–508

Connor, John M. *The Market Power of Multinationals*. New York: Praeger Publishers, 1977.

Cook, Paul, and Colin Kirkpatrick. *Privatization in Less Developed Countries*. New York: St. Martin's Press, 1988.

Country Report on Ghana, Sierra Leone and Libera. London: The Economic Intelligence Unit, Nol 4, 1987.

Cowan, Gray L. "A Global Overview of Privatization." In *Privatization and Development*, edited by Steve H. Hanke, 7. San Francisco, Calif.: International Center for Economic Growth Press, 1987.

De Soto, Hernando. *The Other Path: The Invisible Revolution in The Third World*. New York: Harper and Row, 1989.

DeLancey, Mark W. "Cameroon's Foreign Relations." In *The Political Economy of Cameroon*, edited by Michael G. Schatzberg and I. William Zartman, 189. New York: Praeger, 1986.

Delgado, Christopher, and William Zartman, eds. *The Political Economy of Ivory Coast*. New York: Praeger, 1984.

den Tuinder, Bastiaan A. *Ivory Coast, The Challenge of Success*. Baltimore, Md.: John Hopkins University Press, 1978.

Dewey, John. "Democracy Is a Way of Life." In *Frontiers of Democratic Theory*, 13. Edited by Henry S. Kariel, 13. New York: Random House, 1970.

Diarra, Bakary. Director, Office of Public Sector. Government of Mali, Washington, D.C. Interview, July 16, 1992.

"Discours du Président de la République à l'Occasion du Nouvel An." *Salongo* 2 (January 1974): 1–4.

"Discours du Président Fondateur du Mouvement Populaire de la Revolution à l'Ouverture de l'Institut Makanda Kabobi, le 5 Août 1974." *Etudes Zairoises* 2 (June/July, 1974): 205.

Dobbs, Michael. "Russia Yeltsin Reviles Communist Past, Pledges Better Life for All within a Year." *Washington Post*, 30 December 1991, 10.

Donnison, David. "The Progressive Potential of Privatization." Cited in Michael O'Higgins. "Social Welfare and Privatization: The British Experience." In *Privatization and The Welfare State*, 157. Edited by Alfred J. Kahn and Sheila B. Karmerman, 157. Princeton, N.J.: Princeton University Press, 1989.

Driscoll, David D. *The IMF and The World Bank: How Do They Differ?* Washington, D.C.: International Monetary Fund, 1992.

——. *What is the International Monetary Fund?* Washington, D.C.: International Monetary Fund, 1992.

Dumond, René. *False Start in Africa*. New York: Frederick A. Praeger, 1966.

Dunning, John H, ed. *Multinational Enterprises, Economic Structure and International Competitiveness*. New York: John Wiley & Sons, 1985.

——. *Economic Analysis and the Multinational Enterprise*. London: The Gresham Press, 1974.

Duvall, Raymond, and John A.Freeman, "The State and Dependent Capitalism." *International Studies Quarterly* 25 (1981): 25–105.

Encarnation, Dennis J., and Louis T. Wells, Jr., "Evaluating Foreign Investment." In *Investing in Development: New Roles for Private Capital?* edited by Theodore H. Moran, 61. New Brunswick, N.J.: Transaction Books, 1986.

"Etat d'Avancement du Premier Programme de Privatisation." *Document - Mission de Rehabilitation des Entreprises du Secteur Public et Para Public*, 3–4. Yaounde: Commission Technique, 1993.

Farrell, K. "Public Services in Private Hands." In *Privatization and the Welfare State*, edited by J. LeGrand and R. Robinson. London: Allen & Unwin, 1984.

Federal Reserves. *Regulation K. International Banking Operations*. Washington, D.C.: Federal Reserves Press Release, August 12, 1987.

"Financing Adjustment with Growth in Sub-Saharan Africa 1986–90." *The World Bank Report*. Washington, D.C.: The World Bank, 1986.

"Forces in Zaire Open Fire on Democracy Demonstrators." *Washington Post*, 17 September 1992, p. A33.

Fund-Supported Programs, Fiscal Policy and Income Distribution. Occasional Paper 46. Washington, D.C.: International Monetary Fund, 1986.

Galbraith, John Kenneth. *The New Industrial State*. New York: Signet, Penguin, 1968.

——. *The New Industrial State*. Boston: Houghton Mifflin, 1967.

Gallarotti, Giulio M. "The Limits of International Organization: Systematic Failure in the Management of International Relations." *International Organization* 45 (Spring 1991): 183.

Girvetz, Harry K. *Democracy and Elitism. Two Essays with Selected Readings*. New York: Charles Seribner's Sons, 1967.

Goodman, John B, and Gary W. Loveman, "Does Privatization Serve the Public Interest?" *Harvard Business Review* 69 (November-December 1991): 26–28.

Goodsell, Charles. *The American Corporation and the Peruvian Politics*, Cambridge, Mass.: Harvard University Press, 1974.

Gormley, William T, Jr. "The Privatization Controversy." In *Privatization and Its Alternatives*, 4. edited by William T. Gormley, Jr., 4. Madison: University of Wisconsin Press, 1991.

Gormley, William T. Jr., ed. *Privatization and Its Alternatives*. Madison: University of Wisconsin Press, 1991.

Goulet, Dennis. *Incentives for Development: The Key to Equity*. New York: New Horizon Press, 1989.

———. *Mexico: Development Strategies for the Future*. Notre Dame, Ind.: University of Notre Dame Press, 1983.

———. *The Cruel Choice: A New Concept in the Theory of Development*. New York: Atheneum, 1971.

Graham, Keith. *The Battle of Democracy: Conflict, Consensus and the Individuals*. Totowa. N.J.: Barnes & Noble Books, 1986.

Greene, Joshua, and Delano Villanueva,. *Private Investment in Developing Countries: An Empirical Analysis*. Washington, D.C.: International Monetary Fund, Staff Papers, vol. 31 no. 1,. (June 1984): 379–403.

Grico, Joseph M. "Foreign Investment and Development: Theories and Evidence." In *Investing in Development: New Roles for Private Capital?*, edited by Theodore Moran, 21. New Brunswick: Transaction Books, 1986.

Halton, Richard H., and Brahash S. Sethi, "Management of the Multinationals." Symposium Sponsored by the School of Business Administration of California, Berkeley, July 1972.

Hance, William A. *African Economic Development*. New York: Frederick A. Praeger, 1967.

Hanke, Steve H., ed. *Privatization and Development*. San Francisco, Calif.: International Center For Economic Growth Press, 1987.

Haq, Ul Mahbub. "A View from the South: The Second Phase of the North-South Dialogue." In *The Struggle For Economic Development: Readings in Problems and Policies,* edited by Michael P. Todaro, 385. New York: Longman, 1983.

Harberson John W., and Donald Rothchild, eds. *Africa in World Politics*. Boulder, Colo.: Westview Press, 1991.

Hatry, Harry. *A Review of Private Approaches for Delivery of Public Services*. Washington, D.C.: Urban Institute, 1983.

Heath, John, ed. *Public Enterprises at the Crossroads: Essays in Honour of V.V. Ramanadham*. New York: Routledge, 1990.

Hemming, Richard, and Ali M. Mansoor, "Is Privatization the Answer?" *Finance & Development* 25 (September 1988): 31–33.

Hennessy, Peter. *Whitehall*. New York: Free Press, 1989.

Henry, Neil. "France, Belgium Send Troops to Zaire." *Washington Post*, 25 September 1991, p. A19.

Herrick, Bruce, and Charles P. Kindleberger. *Economic Development*. McGraw-Hill, 1977.

Herschman, A. O. *The Strategy of Economic Development.* New Haven, Conn.: Yale University Press, 1958.

Heydary, Michael. Foreign Minerals Specialist, U.S. Bureau of Mines. Division of International Minerals. Washington, D.C. Interview, October28, 1992.

Hull, Galen S. *Pawns on a Chess Board: The Resource War in Southern Africa.* Washington, D.C.: University Press of America, 1981.

Hunt, Diane. *Economic Theory of Development.* Savage, Md.: Barnes & Noble Books, 1989.

Hymer, Steven. "Study of Direct Foreign Investment, The International Operations of National Firms." Ph.D. dissertation Massachusetts Institute of Technology, 1960.

International Bank for Reconstruction and Development. *Articles of Agreement. Article 1 (ii) and Article III, Section 4 (ii).*

International Finance Corporation, *Annual Report,* Washington, D.C., 1981.

Israel, Arturo. "The Changing Role of the State in Development." *Finance & Development* 28 (June, 1991): 41–43.

Jaffee, David. *Level of Socio-Economic Development Theory.* New York: Praeger, 1990.

Jones, Leroy P., Pankaj Tandon, and Ingo Vogelsang. *Selling Public Enterprises: A Cost-Benefit Methodology.* Cambridge, Mass.: The MIT Press, 1990.

——. *Selling Public Enterprises: A Cost/Benefit Methology.* Cambridge, Mass.: The MIT Press, 1990.

Kainz, Howard P. *Democracy East and West: A Philosophical Overview.* New York: St. Martin's Press, 1984.

Kannyo, Edward. "Colonial Politics in Zaire 1960–1979." In Zaire: The Political Economy of Underdevelopment, edited by Guy Gran, 99. New York: Praeger Publishers, 1979.

Kay, J. A., and D. J. Thompson "Privatization: A Policy in Search of a Rational." *Economic Journal* 96: (March 1986): 18–22.

——."Privatization: A Policy in Search of a Rationale." *Economic Journal* 96 (March, 1986): 18–22.

Kent, Calvin A., "Privatization of Public Functions: Promises and Problems." In *Entrepreneurship and the Privatizing of Government,* edited by Calvin A. Kent, 4. New York: Quorum Books, 1987.

Kent, Calvin A., ed. *Entrepreneurship and the Privatizing of Government.* New York: Quorum Books, 1987.

Kerlin, John J., John C. Ries, and Sidney Sonenblum. "Alternatives to City Departments." In *Alternatives for Delivering Public Services,* edited by E. S. Savas, 111–145. Boulder, Colo.: Westview Press, 1977.

Kesseng, Andre Blaise. Economic Counselor, Embassy of Cameroon. Washington, D.C. Interview, December 7, 1992.

Keynes, John Maynard. *The General Theory of Employment Interest and Money.* New York: Harcout, Brace and Co., 1936.

Killick, T. "Development Planning in Africa: Experiences, Weakness and Prescriptions." *Development Policy Review* 1 (1983): 47–76.

Kirkpatrick, Colin. "Some Background Observation in Privatization." In*Privatization in Developing Countries,* edited by V. V. Ramanadham, 100. London: Routledge, 1989.

——. "Some Background Observations on Privatization." In *Privatization in Developing Countries*, edited by V. V. Ramanadham, 96. London: Routledge, 1989.

Kolderie, T. "Two Different Concepts of Privatiztion." *Public Administrative Review* (July/August 1986): 285–290.

Kpundeh, Sahr John, ed. *Democratization in Africa: Africa View, Africa Voices*. Washington, D.C.: National Research Council, Academy Press, 1993.

——. *Democratization in Africa: Africa View, Africa Voices*. Washington, D.C.: National Research Council, National Academy Press, 1993.

Kulimushi, Nyangezi. Représentant du P.D.G. en Europe. SOZACOM. Brussels. Interview, February 11, 1983.

Landell-Mills, Joslin. *Helping the Poor: The IMF's New Facilities for Structural Adjustment*. Washington, D.C.: International Monetary Fund, 1991.

Leistner, Erich. "Nationalization and Social Justice." *Africa Insight* 20 (1990): 2.

"Les Acquereurs et les Politiciens." *Salongo* 2 (January 1974): 1–2.

"Les Entreprises d'Etat Ont échoué." *Salongo* 2 (July 1974): 2–5.

"Les Acquereurs." *Salongo*, 31 December 1973, p. 2.

"Les Mesures de Zairianisation." *JIWE* 3 (June, 1974): 107–139.

Leonard, Jeffrey. "Multinational Corporations and Politics in Developing Countries." *World Politics* 32, no. 3 (April 1980): 454–483.

Leroy, Jacques. Directeur Division Cuivre. Département Commercial Europe. SOZACOM. Brussels. Interview, February 11, 1983.

Lord, Steve. "Gas and Electricity Shops." In *Privatization?*, edited by Sue Hastings and Hugo Levie, 107. Oxford: Spokesman Books, 1983.

MacGaffey, Janet. "Issues and Methods in the Study of African Economies." In *The Real Economy of Zaire*, edited by Janet MacGaffey, 7. Philadelphia: University of Pennsylvania Press, 1991.

Manning, Brenda, and Clyde Mitchell-Weaver. "Public-Private Partnerships in Third World Development: A Conceptual Overview." *Studies in Comparative International Development* 26 (Winter 1991–1992): 45.

Margolis, Michael. *Viable Democracy*. New York: St. Martin's Press, 1979.

Marketing in Cameroon, Overseas Business Report. Washington, D.C.

Mazur, Robert E., ed. *Breaking the Link: Development Theory and Practice in Southern Africa*. Trenton, N.J.: Africa World Press, 1990.

McCoy, Timothy S., and David H. Shinn, *Democratization and Good Governance in Africa*. Washington, D.C.: Center for Study of Foreign Affairs, Foreign Affairs Institute, U.S. Department of State, May 1992.

McIntosh, Christopher. "Privatization Pundit." *World Development* 4 (January 1991): 28.

McPherson, Peter M. "The promise of Privatization." In *Privatization and Development*, edited by Steve H. Hanke, 18. San Francisco, Calif.: International Center For Economic Growth Press, 1987.

Meyer, Richard T., and Waheb A. Soufi. *Saudi Arabian Industrial Investment: An Analysis of Government-Business Relationships*. New York: Quorum Books, 1991.

Middendorf, William J., Jr., *Implementing the Baker Initiative*. Current Policy No. 781. Washington, D.C.: U.S. Department of State, 1986.

Mikesell, Raymond F. *Foreign Investment in Copper Mining, Case Studies of Mines in Peru and Papua New Guinea*. Baltimore: John Hopkins University Press, 1975.

"Mobutu's Empire of Graft." *Africa Now* 11 (March 1982): 12–23.

Monga, Celestin. "50 Propositions Pour Sauver l'Economie du Cameroon." *Jeune Afrique* 159 (September 1992): 114.

Montagu-Pollock, Matthew. "Privatization What Went Wrong?" *Asian Business* 26 (August 1990): 32–39.

Moore, Richard M. "Alternative Sources of Capital." In *African Debt and Financing*, edited by Carol Lancaster and John Williamson, 148–160. Washington, D.C.: Insitute for International Economics, 1986.

Moran, Theodore H. *Investing in Development: New Roles for Private Capital.* New Brunswick: Transaction Books, 1986.

——. "Transnational Strategies of Protection and Defense by Multinational Corporations, Spreading the Risk and Raising the Cost for Nationalization in Natural Resources." *International Organization* 27 (Spring 1973): 55.

——. *Multinational Corporations and the Politics of Dependence: Copper in Chile.* Princeton, N.J.: Princeton University Press, 1977.

Morley, Samuel P. "The Choice of Technology, Multinational Corporations in Brazil." *Economic Development and Cultural Change* 25, no. 2 (January 1977): 239–64.

Mosley, Paul. "Privatization Policy-Based Lending and World Bank Behaviour." In *Privatization in Less Developed Countries*, edited by Paul Cook and Colin Kirkpatrick, 125–139. New York: St. Martin's Press, 1988.

"Mr. Mobutu's Obligation to Zaire." *Washington Post*, 6 April 1992, p. A12.

Mueller, Willard F., and Richard S. Newfarmer, *Multinational Corporations in Brazil and Mexico, Structural Sources of Economic and Noneconomic Power.* A Report to the Subcommittee on Multinational Corporations on the Committee on Foreign Relations, U.S. Senate Washington, D.C.: Government Printing Office, 1975.

Musgrave, R., and P. Musgrave, *Public Finance in Theory and Practice.* New York: McGraw-Hill, 1984.

Ndongko, Alfred A. "The Political Economy of Development in Cameroon: Relations between the State, Indigenous Business, and Foreign Investors." In *The Political Economy of Cameroon*, edited by Michael G. Schatzberg and I. William Zartman, 83. New York: Praeger, 1986.

Nellis, John R. Public Enterprises in Sub-Saharan Africa. World Bank Discussion Paper No. 1., 32–43. Washington, D.C.: The World Bank, 1986.

Noble, Kenneth B. "Zaire Coalition Ends 26 Years of Dictatorship." *New York Times*, 30 September 1991, p. 2.

Oman, Charles P. "New Forms of Investment in Developing Countries." In *Investing in Development: New Roles for Private Capitals?*, edited by Theodore H. Moran, 131–132. New Brunswick: Transaction Books, 1986.

Pack, Janet Rothenberg. "The Opportunities and Constraints of Privatization." In *Privatization and Its Alternatives*, edited by William T. Gormley, 284. Madison: University of Wisconsin Press, 1991.

Pena, Felix. "Multinational Enterprises and North-South Relations." In *Beyond Dependency, The Developing World Speak Out*, edited by Guy F. Erb and Valariana Kallab, 68–69. New York: Overseas Development Council, 1975.

Penrose, Edith T. "The State and Multinational Enterprises in Less Developed Countries." In *The Multinational Enterprises*, edited by John Dunning. New York: Praeger Publishers, 1971.

Perie, Madsen, and Peter Young. "Development with Aid: Public and Private Responsabilities in Privatization." In *Privatization and Development*, edited by Steve H. Hanke, 175. San Francisco: International Center for Economic Growth Press, 1987.

"Peru's Leader Sets Dates for return to Democracy." *Washington Post*, 22 April 1992, p. A 23.

"Président Mobutu et son Discours sur les Acquereurs." *Salongo* 25 (March 1974): 1–3.

Placca, Jean-Baptiste. "Cameroon, John Fru Ndi en Campagne." *Jeune Afrique* 159 (September 1992): 124.

Poole, R., Jr. "Objections to Privatization." *Policy Review* (Spring 1983): 106–121.

Prayer, Jonas. "Is Privatization a Panacea for LDCs? Market Failure versus Public Sector Failures." *Journal of Development* 26 (April 1992): 301–321.

Preston, P. W. *New Trends in Development Theory: Essays in Dvelopment and Social Theory*. New York: Routledge & Kegan Paul, 1985.

Pryke, Richard. *The Nationalized Industries: Policies and Performance Since 1968*. Oxford: Robert Martin, 1981.

Ramamurti, Ravi. "The Impact of Privatization on the Latin American Debt Problem." *Journal of Interamerican Studies and World Affairs* 34 (Summer 1992): 93–125.

———. "Why Are Developing Countries Privatizing?" *Journal of International Business Studies* 23 (1992): 225–249.

Ramanadham, V. V., ed. *Privatization in Developing Countries*. London: Routledge, 1989.

Richburg, Keith B. "Economic Collapse Withers Lush Zaire." *Washington Post*, 31 March 1992, p. A1.

———."Mobutu: A Rich Man in Poor Standing." *Washington Post*, 3 October 1991, p. A38.

Roberts, Paul Craig. "What Will Set Latin America Free? Free Enterprise." *Business Week* (June 15, 1992): 28.

Sandbrook, Richard. "The State and Economic Stagnation in Tropical Africa." *World Development* 14 (1986): .327

Schatzberg, Michael G. *Politics and Class in Zaire*. New York: Africana Publishing Company, 1980.

Schumpeter, J. *Capitalism, Socialism and Democracy*, 4th edition. London: Unwin, 1954.

———. *The Theory of Economic Development*. Cambridge, Mass.: Harvard University Press, 1934.

Sedibe, Ousmane. Director, Agency For Promotion of Private Enterprise. Government of Mali, Washington, D.C. Interview, July 16, 1992.

Shepherd, George W. *The Trampled Grass: Tributary States And Self-Reliance in the Indian Ocean Zone of Peace*. Westport, Conn.: Greenwood Press, 1987.

Short, R. P. "The Role of Public Enterprises: An International Statistical Comparison." In *Public Enterprise in Mixed Economies: Some Microeconomic Aspects*, edited by Robert H. Floyd et. al., 169. Washington, D.C.: International Monetary Fund, 1984.

Sidelsky, Robert. "The Decline of Keynesian Politics." In *State and Economy in Contemporary Capitalism,*. edited by Colin Crouch, 55–86. London: Croom Helm, 1979.

Sklar, Richard L. *Corporate Power in an African State.* Berkeley: University of California Press, 1975.

Smith, Adam. *An Inquiry into the Nature and Causes of the Wealth of Nations.* New York: The Modern Library, Random House, 1937.

Somjee, A. H. *Development Theory: Critiques and Explorations.* New York: St. Martin's Press, 1991.

Spar, Deborah L., and Raymond Vernon,. *Beyond Globalism: Remaking American Foreign Economic Policy.* New York: Free Press, 1989.

Spero, Joan A. *The Politics of International Economic Relations.* New York: St. Martin's Press, 1977.

Springuel, Rene, ed. *Privatisation en Afrique.* Rapport du PCRP IX. Washington, D.C.: International Development Training Institute, 1991.

"Stabilisation et Reliance Economique: Privatisation des Entreprises." *Cameroon Tribune* 6 (December 1993): 6–9.

Starr, Paul. "The Meaning of Privatization." In *Privatization and the Welfare State,* edited by Alfred J. Kahn and Sheila B. Kamerman, 15. Princeton, N.J.: Princeton University Press, 1989.

Tambunlertchai, Somsak. "Foreign Direct Investment in Thailand's Manufacturing Industry." Ph.D. dissertation, Department of Economics, Duke University, 1975.

Tardy, Patrick. "Painful Adjustments in Africa." *World Press Review* 39 (February 20, 1992): 43.

"The FNLC and the Regime." *Misonga* 3 (June 1978): 11–15.

Thomas, Peter. "The Legal and Tax Considerations of Privatization." In *Privatization and Development,* edited by Steve H. Hanke, 87–91. San Francisco: International Center for Economic Growth Press, 1987.

Toye, J. "Dirigisme and Development Economics." *Cambridge Journal of Economics* 9 (1985): 1–14.

"Update: Zaire." *Africa Report* 37 (July/August 1992): 12.

U.S. Department of Commerce, International Trade Administration. September 1990.

Valahu, Mugur. *The Katanga Circus.* New York: Robert Speller & Sons, 1964.

Vernon, Raymond, ed. *The Promise of Privatization: A Challenge For U.S. Policy.* New York: Council on Foreign Relations Books, 1988.

——. *Sovereignty at Bay: The Multinational Spread of U.S. Enterprise.* New York: Basic Books, 1971.

Viravan, Amnuay. "Privatization: Choices and Opportunities." *Journal of Southeast Asia Business* 7 (Fall 1991): 1–11.

Walker, A. "The Political Economy of Privatization." In *Privatization and The Welfare State,* edited by Alfred J. Kahn and Sheila B. Karmerman, 159. Princeton, N.J.: Princeton University Press, 1989.

Waters, Rufus. "Privatization: A Viable Policy Option?" In *Entrepreneurship and Privatizing of Government,* edited by Calvin A. Kent, 35. New York: Quorum Books, 1987.

William, M. L. "The Extent and Significance of the Nationalization of Foreign-Owned Assets in Developing Countries, 1956–1972." *Oxford Economic Paper* 27 (July 1975): 260–273.

Wilson, Ernest J., III,"Africa, A Rush to Privatize." *New York Times,* 30 July 1987, pp. 27–28.

Wolf, Charles, Jr., "A Theory of Nonmarket Failure: Framework for Implementation Analysis." *Journal of Law and Economics* 4 (1979): 107–139.

World Bank Development Report 1987. Washington, D.C.: The World Bank, 1987.

World Bank: World Development Report. Washington, D.C.: Oxford University Press for the World Bank, 1988.

Zaire, Government Archives. *Labor Force in Katanga.* Document 21. Lubumbashi: Zaire Government Publications, 1960.

Zaire, Government Archives. *How State-Owned Enterprises Failed.* Document 36. Kinshasa: Zaire Government Publications, 1987.

Index

Unemployment, 27
Union Miniere, 90-91
Union Miniere du Haut Katanga, 90, 96
Unit copper cost, 88
United Nations, 89, 105
United Nations General Assembly, 101
United States, 2, 6-15, 28, 30, 33-34,
    42, 51, 65, 100, 118
University graduates, 93
Uranium, 87, 132
U.S. policy toward privatization, 42-43
The U.S. Agency for International
    Development (USAID). See also
    USAID
USAID, 32, 42-43, 49, 54, 112

Venezuela, 23, 32, 55, 65
Vertical integration, 82
Voluntary associations, 12
Volunteers, 6
Voucher system, 15

Wage earnings, 98-99
Wages, 11, 26, 96, 98
Washington, D.C., 38, 121
Wealth, 2, 9, 12-13, 56, 63, 105, 113
Wealth of nations, 25
Wealthy individuals, 7
Welfare programs, 9, 28
Well-being, 11, 16, 21, 131
West Africa, 56
Western assistance, 133
Western donors, 88, 135
Western governments, 42
Western world, 44, 131
Western-oriented economy, 117
Wheat, 118
Working class, 96
World Bank, 5, 10, 32, 34, 47-38, 40,
    43-44, 49, 51, 54, 60, 121, 132
    role of the World Bank, 37-42
The World Bank and IMF
    methods, 37-42
    policy toward privatization, 43-
    46
    responsibilities, 37-42
World economy, 32
World market, 24, 59, 62, 93, 97, 117-
    118, 121, 125, 127, 135

Yeltsin, Boris, 15-16
    privatization in Russia, 15-16
    state-owned enterprises, 15-16
Yoruba, 56

Zaire, 7-11, 29-30, 38, 46, 56-57, 60,
    87-113
    Acquisitors and criteria for
    acquisition, 101, 103-113
    Africanization measures, 90-101
    Convention payments, 97
    Wages and salaries of expatriates,
    99
    Zairianization measures, 101-103
Zambia, 10, 46, 56-58, 77, 90, 95, 102
Zimbabwe, 55

About the Author

JACQUES V. DINAVO is vice president of International Trade Investment Corporation, Inc., a company specializing in international trade and development. Dinavo was an advisor to the Prime Minister of Zaire and teaches seminars at U.S. universities on international trade.